# Leading Kids
# to Books
# through
# PUPPETS

MIGHTY EASY MOTIVATORS

# Leading Kids to Books through PUPPETS

## Caroline Feller Bauer

Illustrated by
**Richard Laurent**

American Library Association
Chicago and London 1997

Design and composition by Dianne M. Rooney in Bembo using QuarkXPress 3.32 on the Macintosh 8500/180

Printed on 55-pound Writer's Natural, a pH-neutral stock, and bound in 12-point coated cover stock by McNaughton & Gunn, Inc.

The paper used in this publication meets the minimum requirements of American National Standard for Information Sciences—Permanence of Paper for Printed Library Materials, ANSI Z39.48-1992. ∞

**Library of Congress Cataloging-in-Publication Data**

Bauer, Caroline Feller
    Leading kids to books through puppets / Caroline Feller Bauer.
        p.    cm. — (Mighty easy motivators)
    Includes bibliographical references.
    ISBN 0-8389-0706-7
    1. Children's libraries—Activity programs—United States. 2. Book talks—United States. 3. Libraries and puppets—United States. 4. Conjuring—United States. 5. Children's literature—Bibliography. I. Title. II. Series: Bauer, Caroline Feller. Mighty easy motivators.
Z718.2.U6B385    1997
027.62'5—dc21                    97-1357

07  06  05  04  03      6  5  4  3  2

For Peter,
who pretends that
he doesn't even mind
sharing his home
with a vast collection
of puppets

# Contents

# Contents

# Acknowledgments

"The Ants" from BEAST FEAST, copyright © 1994 by Douglas Florian, reprinted by permission of Harcourt Brace & Company

"Graham Cracker Animals 1-2-3" reprinted with the permission of Simon & Schuster Books for Young Readers, an imprint of Simon & Schuster Children's Publishing Division from GRAHAM CRACKER ANIMALS 1-2-3 by Nancy White Carlstrom. Text copyright (c) 1989 Nancy White Carlstrom.

"FLOWER-BALLERINAS" TEXT COPYRIGHT (c) 1995 BY BARBARA JUSTER ESBENSEN

"Hello" by A. Spilka from Monkey Write Terrible Letters and other poems published by Boyds Mills Press

"Happy Hiccup to You" reprinted with the permission of Simon & Schuster Books for Young Readers, an imprint of Simon & Schuster Children's Publishing Division from IF YOU'RE NOT HERE, PLEASE RAISE YOUR HAND by Kalli Dakos. Text copyright (c) 1990 Kalli Dakos.

"Fishes' Evening Song" Copyright © 1967 by Dahlov Ipcar. From the book WHISPERING AND OTHER THINGS published by Knopf, Random House. Reprinted by permission of McIntosh and Otis, Inc.

J. Patrick Lewis for "Riddle" and "What Puppets Can Do." Copyright © By J. Patrick Lewis. Used by permission of author, who controls all rights.

# Acknowledgments

"There Was an Old Man" written by: Lori Vicker, West Des Moines, IA

"The Scary Dictionary" Copyright Charles Ghigna

"The Cockroach Sandwich" from the book MAKING FRIENDS WITH FRANKENSTEIN Copyright (c) 1993 Colin McNaughton. Reproduced by permission of Walker Books Ltd, London. Published in the US by Candlewick Press, Cambridge, MA

"No Quacking Allowed" reprinted with permission of the author, Carolyn McNanie Moschopoulos

Not This Bear! written by Bernice Meyers. Used with permission

I AM THE DOG, I AM THE CAT by Donald Hall. Copyright (c) 1994 by Donald Hall. Used by permission of Dial Books for Young Readers, a division of Penguin Books USA Inc.

"The History of the Cockroach" by Rick Walton from WHAT TO DO WHEN A BUG CLIMBS IN YOUR MOUTH. Published by Lothrop, Lee & Shepard, 1995.

# What Puppets Can Do

*J. Patrick Lewis*

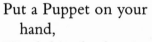

Shadow Puppet,
Finger Puppet,
Puppet on a string—
Puppets do what you
    can do,
Almost *anything!*

Put a Puppet on your
    hand,
Watch him lead a circus band,
Ride a scooter, climb a cliff—
Or blow his nose in a handkerchief!

Pull a Puppet by her strings,
Watch her flap her chicken wings,
Turn and dance. I'll bet two bits
She would even do the splits!

Let your hand make large and small
Moving pictures on the wall.
*Look!* The shadow that you're seeing
Is a Puppet's human being.

If you learn the right technique,
You can speak in Puppetspeak.
So no matter what your age,
*Go ahead and turn the page!*

# Puppets
## *Any Way, Anywhere, Anytime*

It's just a fact of life. Isn't there always a Mary Ann in your class who has gorgeous hair, darling clothes, and can stand on her hands? Well, my "Mary Ann" also had an indulgent daddy who bought her the most amazing toys. She owned a full-size puppet theater that stood in her private playroom. The stage was painted dark blue and studded with sparkling stars. There were crimson velvet curtains that opened and closed when you pulled a golden rope. The marionettes had painted wooden heads and were dressed in silk and sequins.

Although I was completely in awe that a little girl could own such a treasure, we really didn't play with it that much. It was too much trouble to untangle the strings to manipulate the puppets. We argued about who would get to play with the Prince and who would manipulate the Princess. The major reason, I think, that we left it idle was that it was too "ready." There was nothing to make or design; even the plays were already written.

I had my own puppet theater. In fact, I had several. One was constructed from an empty shoe box; a larger theater was a sheet-and-clothesline affair. I had put two nails on either side of the entrance to the study and stretched a clothesline across the opening. When I was a child, sheets came only in white, but crayons helped to decorate the sheet with red and blue stars. Standing behind the sheet, my friends and I could easily hold up the puppets to present a play. I don't remember my parents complaining that I had put nails in the walls or obstructed the entrance to the study or ruined a sheet. No doubt they were furious, but I only remember the fun of putting on a show. And since it was my house, I decided who would play the parts in our puppet play.

Almost anything was useful in our puppet shows. Dolls, stuffed animals, painted hands, kitchen utensils ("Where's the wooden spoon?"), paper dolls, and even our West Highland white terrier found their way into our puppet plays.

Many of the scripts that we used were variations of fairy tales that my mother read to me from Andrew Lang's Color Fairy Tale series. We also made up plays based on popular children's radio programs. Parts of *Superman, Terry and the Pirates,* and *Captain Midnight,* as well as *Lorenzo Jones,* and *Stella Dallas* from the adult radio soap operas, became part of our skits.

This book is meant to reintroduce you and your children to the wonderful world of creative puppet play. It can serve as an overview of several different ways to make puppets and, more importantly, of how to use them to introduce your children to literature.

I have purchased puppets in many countries of the world, Indonesia, China, Turkey, and the local toy store here in the United States, but it still gives me pleasure to fashion a puppet from art materials, stationery supplies, or tools.

Before I became a librarian with a mission to bring books and children together, I often would make a puppet and then wonder what I would do with it. Now I realize that puppets can be a major catalyst in promoting literature.

In this introductory book, I've illustrated several easy-to-make puppets and given examples of how they can perform as part of the literature program.

Think of the many ways that puppets can be used in your program. Their uses for introducing or promoting literature are infinite.

Puppets can

> tell jokes
>
> ask questions
>
> recite poetry
>
> give a booktalk
>
> introduce a friend
>
> announce a new unit of study
>
> explain the rules of the library
>
> ask a riddle
>
> give directions
>
> give rewards
>
> critique an essay
>
> read aloud
>
> tell stories
>
> present a commercial
>
> give a speech
>
> be in a play
>
> narrate a story
>
> teach anything

discuss current affairs

play an instrument

write on the chalkboard

say "hello" or "good-bye" at a program

In Vietnam I had the privilege of attending a water-puppet program. The puppeteers stood behind a screen, knee-deep in water, as they manipulated their puppets on long underwater rods to the music of traditional instruments. When I lived in Salzburg, Austria, I marveled at the full-scale production of Mozart's *Magic Flute* performed by marionettes.

However, the day of puppetry I attended in a local park this summer was the most impressive of all. Members of the Puppet Guild of Greater Miami had organized a day for children in summer school and camp programs. Each guild group brought the puppets that it created and put on skits. Some groups had fully scripted plays; other groups just had their puppets dance to music. In addition, each child had the opportunity to make a puppet to take home at a tent workshop. Professional puppeteers performed with an amazing array of interesting life-size puppets and marionettes. Surely, the children went home and experimented with making and performing with more puppets. And next time? Maybe this year's organizers will have read this book and think in terms of literature-based skits for next year's puppetry festival.

It is my hope that you and your children will make some of the puppets in this book, perform some of the stories and poems, and be inspired to explore the whole idea of bringing literature to children through puppets.

## How *Leading Kids to Books through Puppets* Works

Use the material in this book as a springboard. It is meant to inspire you to bring children and books together using puppets.

>Think Simple.
>
>Think Lively.
>
>Think Fun.
>
>And always . . . Think Books.

True, when you attend a professional puppet show you are awed by the artistry and wonder if using a sock puppet to booktalk a picture book is in the same league. It is not, but remember that pre-schoolers and school-age children will still be thrilled by your personal touch. After all, they are meeting the puppet person up close. Your simple handmade puppet might even be asked to give autographs as a Famous Puppet Person.

*Leading Kids to Books through Puppets* introduces you to some of the basic techniques of puppetry, but its purpose goes beyond puppet performance. You and your children will meet literate puppets who want to show you through the library resources. These puppets like to read, and they want to tell others about their reading interests. They will lead kids to your books.

Following brief instructions on how to create different types of puppets, you will find material to use in performance. In addition, you will find short book lists to remind you of the wealth of materials on the library shelves that can be exhibited or shared with the group.

I hope you will become addicted to puppets, carrying one around with you and being ready to perform in any way, anywhere, anytime, to promote books and reading.

# The Puppet Stage

Try not to be jealous when you visit your friend's kindergarten class and she points to the self-contained puppet stage in the corner and tells you that her uncle Jed made it. Don't be envious when you borrow books from the children's room in the next town and are proudly shown the puppet stage constructed by the librarian's sister-in-law.

Remember that it is not necessary to own or even borrow a fancy puppet theater to enjoy a puppet play. It's possible simply to stand in front of your audience holding and articulating a puppet. Your audience will concentrate on the puppet and won't even see you. In addition, a case can be made for the puppeteer who is in sight of the audience. The audience can see who breathes life into the puppet.

Insist on a stage? Here are some easy-to-fashion stages.

Turn a table
on its side and
kneel behind it.

Fasten a
sheet or
blanket in
a doorway.

Drape a sheet around a hat.

Hold a chalkboard
or bulletin board in
your lap and lean it
against your body.

Cut a
hole in a
refrigerator
carton.

Cut a hole in a book carton, cut out the
back, and place it on a table.

Cut a hole in a box. Cut off the top. Cut off the back to create a top stick-puppet theater.

Cut a hole in a carton. Cut out the bottom
and the back. Put two chairs on a table. Secure
the box between the two chair backs. Drape a
pillow slip or towel from the box to hide the
puppeteer. Use the stage for stick puppets.

See also the shadow-puppet stage on pages 138–39.

# Using Any Type
# of Puppet
# for a Theme

I have moved from country to country, state to state, and street to street. This means that I have packed and boxed my books and puppets at least fourteen times. My conscience says, "Stop buying more puppets. You don't need any more for the rest of your life."

It's still hard for me to resist the puppet tree in a toy or craft shop. I end up with one puppet or more in my luggage each trip. At least I have someone to talk to when I travel. Puppets are great listeners.

At first I tried to buy only the puppets that I needed, but it's not always easy to find what you want, especially if you need to use it tomorrow at 10 A.M. Now I indulge my whims, and I have an extensive collection of puppets with no relation to one another.

You may not be in exactly the same situation, puppets piled all over the beds and bookcases, but if you are a professional working with children, you probably have been tempted and have acquired a hand puppet or two. They are waiting to perform.

In the course of your work, you may have constructed a number of simple puppets with a summer reading group, Scouts troop, or other group. Put them to work.

Here are some examples of theme programs using your choice of puppets.

# A Scary Story, But Not Too Scary

This is a narrative puppet story. A narrator tells the story while manipulating the puppets. Vary the skit according to what puppets are in your collection. Feel free to add or subtract characters depending on how many players you would like to have and how long your skit needs to be.

Encourage the audience members to join in when the lead character is hiccuping. They will enjoy it, and their participation will help you preserve your own voice. An alternative ending to the skit: the elephant loses his hiccups when he is frightened by a little mouse.

**CHARACTERS**

| | |
|---|---|
| Elephant | Princess |
| Queen | Mouse |
| Court Jester | |

**PROPS**

tree

stick puppet of sheep in a huddle (optional)

## Hiccups

Elephant had the hiccups. He sounded like this—audience, please help me demonstrate Elephant's hiccups—Hic . . . Hic . . . Hic . . .

The Queen had an idea. "Elephant, the way to get rid of hiccups is to jump up and down while singing 'Jingle Bells.'"

Elephant tried the Queen's cure. Please help me sing "Jingle Bells" along with Elephant. [Elephant *jumps and sings.*]

The Queen's cure didn't work. Elephant still had the hiccups. Hic . . . Hic . . . Hic . . .

Court Jester had an idea. "Count from one to ten in Spanish while standing on your head."

Elephant tried Court Jester's cure. "Uno, dos, tres, cuatro, cinco, seis, siete, ocho, nueve, diez."

The jester's cure didn't work. Elephant still had the hiccups. Hic . . . Hic . . . Hic . . .

The Princess had an idea. "Close your eyes and recite a nursery song in French."

Elephant tried the Princess's cure.

> Frère Jacques, Frère Jacques
>
> Dormez vous? Dormez vous?
>
> Sonnez les matines,
>
> Sonnez les matines,
>
> Din, din, don
>
> Din, din, don.

The Princess's cure didn't work. Elephant still had the hiccups. Hic . . . Hic . . . Hic . . .

The palace mouse had an idea. "To lose your hiccups, you need to be frightened. Listen to a scary story, but not too scary." Mouse told a story:

"It was a dark and moonless night. Paul was on his way home from work. He had heard about the band of thieves that lurked in the woods, ready to steal from innocent travelers. Paul took the route home through the fields. He wasn't going to be surprised by a band of thieves in the woods. At the tree in the meadow, Paul stopped to rest. [*Bring out tree and place it on the stage or table.*] He lay down and was soon dozing [*snore*]. A sound woke him. He opened his eyes. There, standing around him was the band of thieves. [*hold up sheep*] They were dressed in white and seemed to be praying over him. They probably were praying that there was lots of money to steal. Paul shivered with fright. He jumped up and started to run. And the 'thieves' ran after him, shouting, 'Baaa, Baaa, Baaa!'"

Elephant laughed. The hiccups were gone, scared away by a sheep story.

## More Hiccups

Encourage the audience to join in as your puppet, any puppet from your collection, hiccups in this poem.

### Happy Hiccup to You

*Kalli Dakos*

HICCUP! HICCUP!
"Oh no!" I cried. "This can't be true,
what am I supposed to do?"

HICCUP! HICCUP!
"I have to go out on stage, when the
teacher turns her page."

HICCUP! HICCUP!
"And sing a happy birthday song,
with Fred and Ruth and Matt and John."

HICCUP! HICCUP!
"But I can't sing and hiccup too,
what am I supposed to do?"

HICCUP! HICCUP!
"OH NO! the teacher's turned the page,
now I must go onto the stage."

HICCUP! HICCUP!
"Happy . . . HICCUP . . . to you!
Happy . . . HICCUP . . . to you!
Happy birthday, dear . . . HICCUP!
Happy . . . HICCUP . . . to you!"

("What an awful . . . HICCUP . . . day!")

## Books to Share: Scary, But Not Too Scary

COLLECTIONS

Cecil, Laura. *Boo! Stories to Make You Jump.* Art by Emma Chichester Clark. Greenwillow, 1990. A lavishly illustrated collection of scary stories appropriate for children to read or tell.

Cole, Johanna, and Stephanie Calmenson. *The Scary Book.* Art by Chris Demarest, Marilyn Hirsh, Arnold Lobel, and Dirk Zimmer. Morrow, 1991. Stories and poems for young children. Also perfect for those looking for milder material to tell. "Bony-Legs," "Taily-Po," and "Wait till Martin Comes" are traditional favorites.

Coville, Bruce, ed. *Bruce Coville's Book of Nightmares.* Art by John Pierard. Apple/Scholastic, 1995. One in the series of *Bruce Coville's Book of Monsters, Bruce Coville's Book of Aliens,* and *Bruce Coville's Book of Ghosts.* Scary enough to satisfy young readers, but not so gruesome that adults will worry about their children having nightmares.

Gorog, Judith. *In a Creepy, Creepy Place and Other Scary Stories.* Art by Kimberly Bulcken Root. Harper, 1996. Five stories for young readers featuring the bizarre.

Low, Alice, ed. *Spooky Stories for a Dark and Stormy Night.* Art by Gahan Wilson. Hyperion, 1994.

PICTURE BOOKS

Bender, Robert. *Toads and Diamonds.* Art by the author. Dutton, 1995. Bender has embroidered the Perrault story to include trolls.

Himmelman, John. *Lights Out!* Art by the author. Bridgewater/Troll, 1995. Campers ask Counselor Jim to turn on the lights because they are frightened of assorted monsters.

Pitre, Felix. *Paco and the Witch.* Art by Christy Hale. Lodestar, 1995. A Puerto Rican variant of Rumpelstiltskin, with Spanish vocabulary. Also in Spanish as *Paco y la Bruja.*

San Souci, Robert D. *The Faithful Friend.* Art by Brian Pinkney. Simon, 1995. Two friends on the island of Martinique encounter adventure, love, and zombies.

# Gardens

Use individual flowers as puppets to give booktalks about gardening books. Flowers can be purchased at any variety store. Articulate the flower as it tells about a book. Here is an example:

FLOWER: Good morning. I'm Daffodil. Usually I grow in a park or in front of some- one's house. In *Flower Garden* I travel from a store on a bus to a little girl's apartment. I am going to be a birthday present and live in a box hanging on a windowsill. I'll have a view of the city.

The following little play is another lead-in to gardening books.

**CHARACTERS**

Marvin          Martha

(Use any two puppets of your choice.)

**PROPS**
signs: "Marvin's House," "Library," "Empty Lot"
books about gardens
tinsel
artificial flowers
clay stands (optional)

## Marvin and Martha Plant a Garden

### Scene 1

In front of Marvin's house
[*Hold up sign "Marvin's House."*]

MARVIN: Look what I found—a package of seeds.

MARTHA: Let's make a garden.

MARVIN: How do you do it?

MARTHA: I'm not sure, but there must be directions on the package.

MARVIN: Let me see. It only says, "Compliments of Roger's Dry Cleaning."

MARTHA: We can go to the library. They have books on how to grow a garden.

### Scene 2

Library
[*Hold up sign "Library."*
*Pile garden books on stage.*]

MARVIN: I had no idea that there were so many books about gardens. There are books on where to grow a garden, how to grow a garden, what to grow, when to grow it, and how to cook the vegetables that you grow.

MARTHA: And look at these books. They are all about people who grow gardens in the country and even in the city.

MARVIN: I see that we have a problem. We don't know if these seeds are carrots, beans, radishes, lettuce, or squash. I hate squash.

MARTHA: Don't worry. I'm sure that the seeds are something yummy to eat. Let's go home and follow the directions for growing carrots.

## Scene 3

Empty lot
[*Hold up sign "Empty Lot."*]

MARVIN: Here is a good place to plant the seeds. Help me dig up the earth.

MARTHA: Let's sprinkle the seeds in the ground.

MARVIN: Now we have to wait for the seeds to grow.

MARTHA: Nothing is happening.

MARVIN: We have to wait a long time. We need to water the seeds.

MARTHA: Here comes the rain. It will water the seeds. [Marvin *shakes the tinsel to represent rain.*]

MARVIN: Here comes the sun. There are little weeds in our garden. I'll pull them up.

MARTHA: Nothing is happening.

MARVIN: We need to wait a long time.

MARTHA: Do you think that the seeds are scared of the dark? It must be very dark underground.

MARVIN: I don't think so, but maybe the seeds are lonely. Let's read them a story.

MARTHA: Since they are carrots, let's read *The Carrot Seed*.

MARVIN: I'll go to the library and check it out.

## Scene 4

Marvin's house
[*Hold up sign "Marvin's House."*]

MARTHA: I can't believe that we were in the middle of growing carrots when I was invited to vacation at my aunt Gert's and you were invited to go fishing with your dad.

MARVIN: I can't wait to see if the carrots came up. I'm hungry for a crisp carrot.

MARTHA: Let's go see the garden.

## Scene 5

Empty lot
[*Hold up sign "Empty Lot."*
*Hold up artificial flowers or place them in clay stands on stage. The more you have, the more impressive the scene.*]

MARTHA: Where did all the flowers come from? Where are the carrots?

MARVIN: I think our seeds were for flowers, not carrots.

MARTHA: Let's each take a bouquet of flowers home. My mom always has carrots in the fridge.

MARVIN: My dad will laugh. We didn't catch any fish on our trip, but I said that when we got home we could eat carrots. I don't even think he likes carrots, but he loves flowers.

MARTHA: We should bring some flowers to the library. The library's books helped us grow these carrots—I mean flowers.

## Books to Share: Gardens

Appelt, Kathi. *Watermelon Day.* Art by Dale Gottlieb. Holt, 1996. Jesse watches a watermelon grow all summer and helps enjoy it during the family's reunion.

Brisson, Pat. *Wanda's Roses.* Art by Maryann Cocca-Leffler. Boyds/Mill, 1994. Everyone in the neighborhood helps with the garden in the empty lot.

Bunting, Eve. *Flower Garden.* Art by Kathryn Hewitt. Harcourt, 1994. A little girl plants a window flower box for her mother's birthday.

Butterworth, Nick, and Mike Inkpen. *Jasper's Beanstalk.* Art by the authors. Bradbury, 1993. A cat works to grow a beanstalk every day of the week.

Cole, Henry. *Jack's Garden.* Art by the author. Greenwillow, 1995. Cumulative story and double-spread art show Jack's garden from garden tools to blooming flowers.

DiSalvo-Ryan, DyAnne. *City Green.* Art by the author. Morrow, 1994. Mr. Hammer, hard as nails, plants a surprise in the neighborhood garden plot.

Gerstein, Mordicai. *Daisy's Garden.* Art by Susan Yard Harris. Hyperion, 1995. Planting and harvesting from April to September.

Hall, Zoe. *It's Pumpkin Time!* Art by Shari Halpern. Scholastic, 1994. Children plant a pumpkin patch.

Howard, Ellen. *The Big Seed.* Art by Lillian Hoban. Simon, 1993. Little Bess grows a big flower.

King, Elizabeth. *Backyard Sunflower.* Photographs by the author. Dutton, 1993. Photo-essay showing the life cycle of sunflowers.

Lobel, Arnold. "The Garden." In *Frog and Toad Together.* Art by the author. Harper, 1972. Toad tries his hand at gardening, the classic story featuring Frog and Toad.

Madenski, Melissa. *In My Mother's Garden.* Art by Sandra Speidel. Little, 1995. Rosie plants a birthday surprise for her mother.

Peteraf, Nancy J. *A Plant Called Spot.* Art by Lillian Hoban. Doubleday, 1993. Care of a plant teaches Teddy to take care of a pet.

Velghe, Anne. *Wildflowers.* Art by the author. Farrar, 1994. Flowers are shown painted in their natural setting and identified on the adjacent page.

Wolff, Ferida. *The Emperor's Garden.* Art by Kathy Osborn. Tambourine, 1994. Villagers plant a garden as a present for the emperor.

# A Dictionary Opener

You can use this little motivator with any two puppets. Puppets can perform on a big fat dictionary as their stage.

**PROPS** (optional)
sign with title and poet's name, to display
adding-machine tape with long and short words, to unfurl

## The Scary Dictionary

PUPPET 1:  The Scary Dictionary

PUPPET 2:  By Charles Ghigna
          [*Display the sign with title and poet's name.*]

PUPPET 1:  The biggest book you'll ever see
          Lives deep inside the library!

PUPPET 2:  Alone it sits upon the stand;
          your ticket to a magic land.

PUPPET 1:  Don't be afraid. Don't try to hide.
          Just open it and look inside.

PUPPET 2:  It's really fun to find a word.
          It may be one you've never heard.

PUPPET 1:   It may be long. It may be short.
               It may be just your favorite sport.

PUPPET 2:   So get on your mark and get set.
               It's time to play the alphabet!

PUPPET 1:   You see it isn't very scary . . . .

BOTH PUPPETS:   It's just the dictionary!
     [*Unfurl the long tape with words written on it.*]

PUPPETS CAN HOLD EDGES OF SCROLL

SUPERCALIFRAGILISTICEXPIALIDOCIOUS!

**Books to Share: Word Books**

Here's a chance to introduce your group to dictionaries. If you have children's foreign-language dictionaries available, they too will be interesting for your group to browse.

*The Dorling Kindersley Children's Illustrated Dictionary.*
Illustrated with color photos. Dorling Kindersley, 1994. Twelve thousand words and 2,500 photos make this children's dictionary an excellent introduction to pleasurable reference.

Scarry, Richard. *Richard Scarry's Best Word Book Ever.*
Art by the author. Western, 1963. Best-loved picture dictionary for young children.

*Scholastic Children's Dictionary.* Illustrated with drawings. Scholastic, 1996. Words and labeled drawings for words, maps, and flags too.

# *Turtles*

Wear a turtleneck sweater. You, the narrator, represent the turtle. Use any puppets from your own collection. Adapt the script to the puppets you choose.

As a one-person show, simply pick each puppet up in turn and speak. If you want to involve others, assign parts so that each character has a chance to perform.

If you don't want your players to have to learn formal lines, you can narrate while they simply hold their puppets.

**CHARACTERS**

Turtle

Dog

Cat

Other characters of your choice

## Home

Turtle was slowly making his way through the garden when out from behind a bush jumped Dog.

"Hurry, Turtle. There is going to be a storm; you better get home as fast as possible."

"Don't worry about me," said Turtle. "I'll be home in time."

Turtle plodded slowly, walking through the garden.

Cat bounced by Turtle. "Hurry, Turtle. There is going to be a storm; you better get home as fast as possible."

"Don't worry about me," said Turtle. "I'll be home in time."

*[At this point, add as many different characters as you want. Each character warns of the approaching storm. This is a fantasy, so you don't have to worry if the king or elephant puppet you own lives in the garden where we find Turtle. After the last character appears and you are ready to end your skit, finish it in the following way:]*

Turtle stretched his neck to the sky. His neighbors were right. The storm had arrived. It was starting to rain.

"Time to go home," he said, and he pulled his head into his shell. "I'm home!"

*[Hide your head under the turtleneck of your sweater.]*

## Books to Share: Turtles

Bauer, Caroline Feller. "Terrific Turtles." In *Celebrations*. Art by Lynn Bredeson. Wilson, 1993. Read-aloud program of stories, poems, and activities.

DeSpain, Pleasant. *Eleven Turtle Tales*. Art by Joe Shlichta. August House, 1994. Turtle tales from around the world.

Hirschi, Ron. *Turtle's Day*. Photos by Dwight Kuhn. Dutton, 1994. Introduces a turtle through short text and clear photos.

Katz, Avner. *Tortoise Solves a Problem*. Art by the author. Harper, 1993. Tortoise designs the perfect house for turtles.

Mayo, Margaret. *Tortoise's Flying Lesson*. Art by Emily Bolam. Harcourt, 1994. Eight animal stories, including the tortoise and the hare tale. Share the colorful art.

Mollel, Tololwa M. *The Flying Tortoise: An Igbo Tale*. Art by Barbara Spurll. Clarion, 1994. Tortoise asks the birds to help him fly in this Nigerian story.

Ross, Gayle. *How Turtle's Back Was Cracked*. Art by Murv Jacob. Dial, 1995. In this Cherokee tale, Turtle tries to outwit the wolves.

Staub, Frank. *Sea Turtles*. Photos by the author. Lerner, 1995. Photo-essay focuses on saving sea turtles.

Stoddard, Sandol. *Turtle Time*. Art by Lynn Munsinger. Houghton, 1995. Turtle bedtime story in rhyme.

Wood, Douglas. *Old Turtle.* Art by Cheng-Khee
Chee. Pfeifer-Hamilton, 1992. The message of
peace is delivered by Old Turtle.

Yeoman, John. *The Singing Tortoise.* Art by Quentin
Black. Tambourine, 1993. How Turtle got his
shell and the title story feature turtles.

# Stuffed Animals
## as Puppets

Do you have a favorite stuffed animal who lives on your bed? Or do your children have vast collections of animals that are overtaking beds, floors, and windowsills? Put those plush toys to work. They can be ready-made puppets for telling stories, presenting poetry, or giving booktalks.

One way of turning a stuffed animal into a puppet is to split the back seam and remove the body stuffing. You now have an instant hand puppet. Put your hand into the animal's cavity and you're ready to perform.

The best thing about a stuffed animal, however, is that you don't have to remove the stuffing and destroy your best friend. A stuffed animal is already a puppet. Simply articulate your animal by making it walk or use its paws, "playing" with it just the way you did when you were seven—or just last week in the toy shop.

# The Teddy Bear

Bears are good puppet characters for introducing books in general or for presenting stories, booktalks, and poetry featuring bears. Try the following story, which is fun to present when several players hold stuffed bears that react to the story as told by the narrator. It can also be easily scripted with Herman and the bear family speaking the lines. If you have a large group of children who brought bears from home and are eager to be involved, simply increase the size of the bear family and let the children participate by applauding and laughing with the story. Herman, the boy, can be played by a live actor. The fur coat and hat can be real fur or the boy can be dressed in a furry blanket. Herman should act out the directions of the

narrator. Herman can run to the narrator and hug her at the end of the story.

**CHARACTERS**

Herman, a little boy, dressed in fur hat and coat or a furry blanket

Bear family (at least five bears): Papa, Mama, Big Brown Bear, Baby, a big black burly bear to chase Herman at the end

**PROPS**

fur coat and hat or a furry blanket

table set with dishes and soup bowls

spoon and fork for Herman

# Not This Bear!

*Bernice Myers*

Little Herman went to visit his aunt Gert. He got off the bus at the last stop. But he still had a short walk to her house. It was very, very cold. And to keep warm, Herman pulled himself deeper inside his long furry coat. And he pulled his big furry hat down over his face. He looked just like a bear—which is funny, because that is exactly what a passing bear thought he looked like.

"Look who I found at the edge of the woods!" he shouted. All the bears ran over and kissed Herman hard and wet.

"Cousin Julius, Cousin Julius!" they shouted.

"My name is Herman," said Herman. But no one even heard. They were so excited.

"I'm not a bear . . . ," Herman said.

"Dinner is ready," Mama Bear called. "Take your places. Cousin Julius, you sit here."

When Mama Bear served the soup, all the bears lapped it up with their tongues. But not Herman. He ate politely with a spoon that he happened to have in his pocket.

And when the vegetables were served, Herman ate with a fork that he happened to have in his pocket. The bears were amazed.

"My, my!" Big Brown Bear stared at Herman. "How smart you are to learn a trick like that."

And all the bears clapped as if they were watching a circus act. Poor Herman. He wasn't a bear. He was a little boy. He was sure of it. But the bears were just as sure that Herman was their cousin Julius.

"So," thought Herman, "I'll just prove I'm really a boy!" He began to sing and dance and whistle, tie his shoelace, and stand on his head— all the things a boy knows how to do.

But whatever he did, the bears still thought Herman was a bear. And they clapped even harder at his tricks.

"See what happens," said Papa, "when a bear has a chance to go to the big city and learn a trade."

"What a clever cousin we have," said Big Brown Bear. And he yawned and went outside. Big Brown Bear looked at the sky and announced the time of year—winter.

"After Mom's big meal, we won't eat again until spring," he said. And all the bears got ready to sleep.

"Remember, we sleep for at least two months," said Big Brown Bear.

"Two months!" said Herman, "I only sleep one night at a time. During the day I go out and play. *I'm* not sleeping through the winter."

"But all bears do," said Baby Bear.

"Not *this* bear," answered Herman. "I like winter," he said.

"He likes winter," said the bears, astonished.

"Yes, I like winter. I like to go sledding and to skate. I like to make snowmen and drink hot cocoa with whipped cream. I like snowball fights with my friends, and I like to make giant tracks in the snow. And besides, I have to go to school."

When Herman finished speaking, there was a long silence. Then Big Brown Bear spoke: "Perhaps you aren't a bear after all. In fact, now that I look closer, you don't even have a nose like a bear."

"Look!" shouted a bear, removing Herman's furry hat and coat. "He's not a bear at all."

There, shivering in the cave, stood little Herman. "See, I *am* a boy," he said.

Papa Bear roared with laughter. "That's the best trick of all. And the trick was on us."

Herman put on his furry hat and coat again. He said good-bye to all the bears.

"Come and visit us in spring," they yawned after him.

"I will," he answered, just to be polite. Herman began to walk toward Aunt Gert's house.

He was almost out of the woods when a big black burly bear jumped out from behind a tree. Running toward Herman, the bear shouted, "Cousin Bernard, Cousin Bernard . . .."

But Herman ran just as fast as he could out of the woods. Herman was glad when he finally reached Aunt Gert's porch.

And Aunt Gert was very glad to see Herman.

**More Teddy Bear Books
to Use with Stuffed Animals**

I have used these books with various stuffed bears in many schools around the world. Even children whose English is minimal understand the story if they can see the action as performed by the main character: a bear.

Douglass, Barbara. *Good as New.* Art by Patience Brewster. Lothrop, 1982. When his cousin KC plays with Grady's bear and gets it dirty, Grandpa washes and repairs it.

*Puppetry Tip*

There are three options. Tell the story holding the bear and demonstrating how Grandpa takes the stuffing out of the bear before it is washed, or just show the clean bear at the end. A third option would be to show a decrepit dirty bear at the beginning of the story and a squeaky-clean bear at the end.

Hale, Irina. *Brown Bear in a Brown Chair.* Art by the author. Atheneum, 1983. A brown stuffed bear is constantly being sat upon because he is the same color as the chair.

*Puppetry Tip*

To tell this with a teddy, you will also need some props—a brown bear; a brown chair, or a bear-brown cloth draped over any chair; clothes for the bear, perhaps the same clothes you used with *How Do I Put It On?,* below; and a flowered cloth to re-cover the chair and a dress of the same fabric for the bear to wear. Manipulate the bear as the story unfolds.

Murphy, Jill. *Peace at Last*. Art by the author. Dial, 1980. Papa Bear can't fall asleep because of the disturbing sounds around the house: his wife's snoring, the water dripping from the kitchen sink, and the cuckoo clock in the living room.

### *Puppetry Tip*

Hold the bear prone as though he were asleep. Each time you and the children imitate the sounds that Papa Bear hears, tilt him to a surprised sitting position.

Watanabe, Shigeo. *How Do I Put It On?* Art by Yasuo Ohtomo. Collins, 1979. A small bear puts on his clothes the wrong way—shoes on his ears and his cap on his feet.

### *Puppetry Tip*

Your teddy bear will need clothes to wear in this story. If you are not an accomplished seamstress or tailor or don't have a talented friend to help, purchase clothes that fit your bear in the baby department of a discount store. It will be a memorable shopping expedition as you carry your bear asking for help "to dress my bear" from an astonished clerk. Dress the bear as the story dictates while your audience laughs and shouts instructions.

# Dog and Cat Presentations

This excerpt from a longer book works with any dog or cat. In fact, if you don't have access to a dog and cat, use your favorite stuffed animals and tell your audience that your "elephant" and "dragon" are acting as a dog and a cat. Try to imagine how a dog and cat might talk.

## I Am the Dog, I Am the Cat

*Donald Hall*

### Scene 1

CAT: Dogs are nervous and well-meaning
It is well-known that cats
are at the same time
independent,
selfish,
fearless,
beautiful,
cuddly,
scratchy,
and intelligent.

DOG: Cats just don't *care*.
Only a dog
is at the same time
dignified, guilty, sprightly,
obedient,
friendly,
vigilant,
and soulful.

## Scene 2

CAT: When babies come into the house,
I try to *vanish*.
Babies are crazy!
Babies *sit* on you!

DOG: Making the acquaintance of babies,
I allow them to pull my hair.
I do not like it,
but I allow it, for
I am the dog.

## Scene 3

DOG: I sleep all day in order to stay rested,
in order to be alert
when it is my duty to bark.

CAT: I sleep all day
in order to stay awake all night
on mouse patrol.

DOG: After I sleep all day,
I sleep all night, for
I am the dog.

CAT:  Cats work hard.
        When people and dogs are asleep,
        I never stop hunting mice.
        In the absence of mice,
        I hunt pieces of paper, paper clips,
           or rubber bands.

DOG:  I am the Dog.
CAT:  I am the Cat.

Let your plush dog help you present this poem.

### Hello

*Arnold Spilka*

I taught my dog to say "Hello"
And now he says hello all day,
Hello hello hello hello
That's all I ever hear him say!
When I go out
He says "Hello"

When I come in
He says "Hello"
When I wake up
He says "Hello"
When I'm in bed
He says "Hello"
And now I try
and try
and try
and try
But I just can't teach him to say
    "Goodbye"!

The audience can participate at the end of this traditional rhyme by meowing like a cat and squeaking like a frightened mouse.

### Pussy Cat

Pussy cat, Pussy cat,
Where have you been?
I've been up to London
To look at the queen.

Pussy cat, Pussy cat,
What did you do there?
I frightened a little mouse
Under her chair.

# *Animal Sounds*

Children love to participate in a story by making animal noises. They get their chance when puppets tell this story by Carolyn McNanie Moschopoulos, a teacher at the Harare International School in Zimbabwe.

Hold a stuffed duck as you tell the story. When the duck speaks, cradle it in both hands and move it up and down. You might want to add an actor to say Mom's lines.

Your audience can contribute the sounds of animals and the vacuum cleaner. If your audience members speak different languages, you will hear different ways that animal sounds are interpreted around the world.

## SOUNDS FOR AUDIENCE PARTICIPATION

| | |
|---|---|
| duck | dog |
| vacuum cleaner | cow |
| cat | song that duck sings |

## CHARACTERS

| | |
|---|---|
| Duck | Mother (optional) |

# No Quacking Allowed

*Carolyn McNanie Moschopoulos*

Today Theodore went to the park. He went to see the ducks and throw them some bread. A big white duck sat in his lap, so he decided to take it home. He carried it the whole way in his arms. It was a long, long way.

When Theodore finally got home, he and the duck sat down on the stoop to rest. The duck looked up at Theodore.

"Quack," it said.

"I love you, too," said Theodore with a smile. "Let's go ask Mommy if I can keep you."

He picked up the duck and went inside. His mother was in the kitchen washing some pots and pans.

"Hi, Mom—look what I found in the park. Can I keep him, Mom, please, oh please?"

"Quack, quack," said the duck happily.

His mom looked down at Theodore. Her eyes got bigger and bigger, and her mouth opened wider and wider, before she said anything.

"Quacking? Oh, no, Theodore! Get that duck out of here. I can't have the duck quacking around the house all day. He'll drive me crazy!"

Theodore turned sadly away and went back outside. He and the duck sat down to figure out what to do.

Suddenly the duck stretched up and whispered in Theodore's ear. Theodore jumped up and ran back into the house.

His mother was vacuuming the living room rug. "Mom, Mom!" yelled Theodore over the noise of the vacuum. She shut it off.

"Mom, Mom, can I keep him now?"

The duck turned to Theodore's mother, opened his bill, and in a clear, clean voice began to bark.

"Arf! Arf! Arf!"

"No!" his mother cried, throwing up her hands in horror. "I can't have a duck barking around the house all day. What will the neighbors say?"

Theodore sadly carried the duck outside again. They sat on the stoop and began to think. Suddenly the duck stretched up and whispered something in Theodore's ear. Up jumped Theodore, and rushed back into the house.

His mother was sitting on the couch reading the newspaper.

"Mom, Mom, do you like him now, huh, Ma, can I keep him?"

The duck turned toward Theodore's mother, opened his bill, and in a clear, loud voice began to meow.

"Meow, meow, meow."

"Oh no!" cried his mother. "I can't have a duck meowing around the house all day. We'll attract all the dogs in the neighborhood!"

Once again Theodore and the duck went out on the stoop. "I'll never be able to keep you," he said sadly, and he hugged the duck closer to him.

The duck seemed to think for a minute or
two and then stretched up to whisper something
in Theodore's ear. Theodore looked at the duck,
shook his head, and said, "All right, we'll try."

He carried the duck back into the house,
where he found his mother on her way upstairs.
She was holding the banister with one hand; she
held the other hand to her head.

"Ma," said Theodore.

"Theodore, now I have a headache," said his
mother, "and I'm going upstairs to lie down."

"Ma, could we maybe possibly just this once
keep him now?"

The duck turned to Theodore's mother,
opened his bill and, in a clear, deep
voice, began to moo.

"Moo. Moo. Moo."

"No, Theodore. I have a
headache, Theodore. No moo-
ing, please. Take that duck back
to the park."

Back on the stoop Theodore
thought he was going to cry. The
duck curled up and sadly laid his head
across his back feathers. The two of
them had been sitting there for at least
five minutes when suddenly the duck
jumped off Theodore's lap, stood up straight and
tall, and leaned over to whisper in Theodore's
ear.

"It'll never work!" he cried. "She told me to
take you back to the park." Once again the duck
whispered in Theodore's ear. Theodore began to

smile. "You really think we should try? All right, come on!"

Theodore grabbed the duck and ran straight into the house and up the stairs, where he found his mother stretched out on the bed, an ice bag on her head. "No," she moaned when she saw Theodore standing there with the duck. "Get him out of here! Oh, my aching head."

"Please, Ma, just this last time. Please!"

As Theodore and his mother were arguing, the duck leaped out of Theodore's arms, waddled up onto the bed, opened his bill, and in a clear voice began to sing.

"La. La. La. La."

The duck sang song after soft sweet song, and slowly Theodore's mother's eyes began to close, and she fell peacefully asleep.

Theodore got to keep the duck, whom he named Caruso after a famous singer.

Whenever Theodore's mother was around, Caruso sang his soft sweet songs. But as soon as he and Theodore were alone, Caruso quacked and quacked, like the happy duck he was.

## Books to Share

DUCKS

Brenner, Barbara, and Julia Takaya. *Chibi: A True Story from Japan.* Art by June Otani. Clarion, 1996. A duck family makes its home in busy Tokyo.

Flack, Marjorie. *Angus and the Ducks*. Art by the author. Doubleday, 1932. The ducks hiss at the Scottie in this childhood classic.

Grindley, Sally. *Peter's Place*. Art by Michael Foreman. Harcourt, 1996. After an oil spill, Peter helps with the cleanup. His special duck survives.

Gordon, Gaelyn. *Duckat*. Art by Chris Gaskin. Scholastic, 1992. In this story, a duck thinks it's a cat.

McCloskey, Robert. *Make Way for Ducklings*. Art by the author. Viking, 1941. Two mallard ducks find a home in Boston.

Waddell, Martin. *Farmer Duck*. Art by Helen Oxenbury. Candlewick, 1992. Duck is overworked until his friends help to outwit the lazy farmer.

## MIXED-UP ANIMAL SOUNDS

Causeley, Charles. *"Quack!" Said the Billy-Goat*. Art by Barbara Firth. Harper, 1986. The barnyard animals make all the wrong noises when Farmer Brown lays an egg.

Forrester, Victoria. *The Magnificent Moo*. Art by the author. Atheneum, 1983. A cow trades her moo for the cat's meow.

Root, Phyllis. *One Windy Wednesday*. Art by Helen Craig. Candlewick, 1996. The wind blows so hard that it blows the animals' sounds all over the farm.

Zimmerman, Andrea, and David Clemesha. *The Cow Buzzed*. Art by Paul Meisel. Harper, 1993. The bee has a cold, and all the farm animals catch it and one another's sounds, too.

# Catalog Puppets

**A**re you drowning in department store or thematic mail-order catalogs? These unsolicited booklets are an instant source of puppets. Instead of throwing the catalogs away or spending money ordering something that you may not need or even want, use the glossy photographs of people and things to create individual stick puppets.

**YOU WILL NEED**
pictures or photos of a variety of people cut from mail-order catalogs
Popsicle sticks (available at a grocery store or craft shop) or tongue depressors (available at a pharmacy)
cellophane tape

**PREPARATION**
Use cellophane tape to hold the sticks to the back of the picture. Laminate the pictures if you want them to last forever!

## PERFORMANCE

Catalog puppets bring out the best in young performers. The children gain confidence by holding on to a puppet, but the puppets are so small that the performer is in full view of the audience.

My daughter used catalog puppets with her students when she was teaching English in a Japanese middle school. The students were good at writing and reading English, but were painfully shy about speaking it. The catalog puppets enabled them to pretend that it was the puppet doing the talking, and not them. After all, it's okay for a puppet to make a mistake in grammar or forget a vocabulary word.

These catalog puppets can ask each other factual questions or even sometimes answer "real-life" questions with more candor than their human hosts.

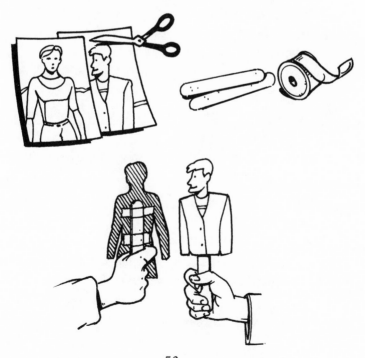

## Questions Puppets
## Can Ask Each Other

What do you think?

If you were president of the United States, what would you change?

If you were the principal of your school, what would you change?

If a space alien visited your town, what would you show it?

If you could buy anything in the world, what would you buy?

If you were mayor of your town, what changes would you suggest?

What is your favorite holiday? Why?

If you were granted one wish, what would you wish (no wishing for more wishes)?

If you could be changed into an animal, what animal would you choose?

If you could travel anywhere in the world, where would you go? Why?

Do you think boys and girls are different?

What makes a good friend?

What is your favorite season? Why?

If you were changed into one of your parents, would you do things differently?

Would you rather be rich or famous?

If you could take only one book with you to a desert island, which book would you choose?

If you were leaving your home forever and could choose just one thing to take with you, what would you choose?

## Proverbs in English, Spanish, and French

To a pair of conversing puppets, add one more puppet to perform these proverbs in three languages. Can you think of other proverbs, in any language?

Clothes don't make the man.
El hábito no hace la persona.
L'habit ne fait pas le moine.

Better late than never.
Más vale tarde que nunca.
Mieux vaut tard que jamais.

All that glitters is not gold.

Todo lo que brilla no es oro.

Tout ce qui brille n'est pas or.

Two heads are better than one.

Cuantos cabezas, tantos pareceres.

Deux avis valent mieux qu'un.

One swallow does not a summer make.

Una golondrina no hace verano.

Une hirondelle ne fait pas le printemps.

His bark is worse than his bite.

Perro que ladra no muerde.

Chien qui aboie ne mord pas.

## Books to Share

PROVERBS

Hurwitz, Johanna, ed. *A Word to the Wise and Other Proverbs*. Art by Robert Rayevsky. Morrow, 1994. A collection of proverbs illustrated with wit.

*"Too Many Cooks . . ." and Other Proverbs*. Art by Maggie Kneen. Green Tiger, 1992. Animals show young readers traditional proverbs.

ADULT SOURCE

Stevenson, Burton Egbert. *The Home Book of Proverbs, Maxims and Familiar Phrases*. Macmillan, 1948. Contains seventy-three thousand expressions from many languages and periods.

# Partner Puppets
# for Riddlers

Rather than thinking in terms of a full-blown play production with an audience, let your children pick a partner for puppet exchanges of riddles. Riddles are so popular with children that you won't even have to create or find material to use with your puppets. You can use the riddles here to spark the children's memory, but once you ask a riddle or two, your group will suddenly have full recall of a whole program of riddles. But don't feel you have to do a complete program. If you have ever had second or third graders badger you with their repertoire, you know how tedious riddles can be when overdone. Use the riddles as introductory material or as transitional material between activities.

# *Paper Mouth*
# *Puppets*

Easy-to-make paper mouth puppets are perfect to use with riddles where the action is in the words rather than physical movement. Children enjoy making these puppets because they do not take much time and yet are effective presentation partners. Sometimes we put a lot of effort into creating a puppet and then are stymied about what to do with it. There seem to be an endless number of riddle books that will thrill children while they choose their favorites to show each other.

Here's how to make and decorate these paper mouth puppets:

## 1. Fold-up puppet

Fold a standard sheet of construction paper or a longer sheet, 10″ x 17″, first into thirds, lengthwise; then into quarters. Top and bottom should meet in the middle. Fold in half again, with the openings on the outside. Work your thumb and fingers into the slots to animate the "mouth."

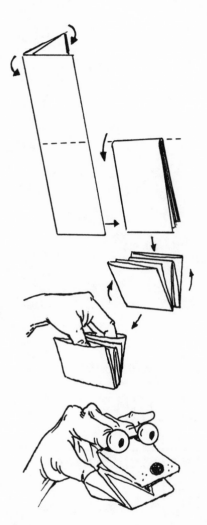

## 2. Paper-plate mouth puppet

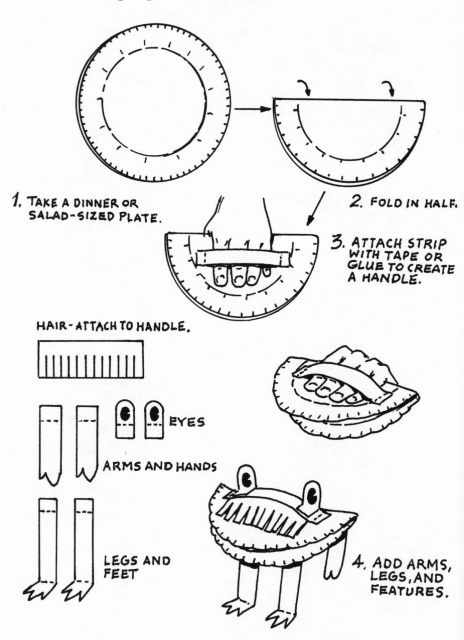

1. TAKE A DINNER OR SALAD-SIZED PLATE.

2. FOLD IN HALF.

3. ATTACH STRIP WITH TAPE OR GLUE TO CREATE A HANDLE.

HAIR - ATTACH TO HANDLE.

EYES

ARMS AND HANDS

LEGS AND FEET

4. ADD ARMS, LEGS, AND FEATURES.

## Riddle

*J. Patrick Lewis*

The seven strings above my head
Can wake me up, put me to bed.

Or make me dance a little jig—
I zig and zag and zag and zig.

My arms can swing, my toes can point,
My body jumps from every joint

Because someone is in the wings—
Behind the curtain pulling strings.

*a marionette*

# Paper Puppet
# Portraits

A portrait on paper can be used as a hand puppet to introduce a biography. The portraits can be of the biographical subjects drawn by you or your children, or they can simply represent generic readers as in the patterns provided.

# *Biographical Sketches: Tell a Life*

**YOU WILL NEED**

paper

crayons

scissors

rubber cement or
a Band-Aid

Popsicle stick

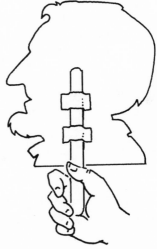

**PREPARATION**

Draw a face on typing or
drawing paper. Glue the
drawing to the palm of the
puppeteer's hand with rubber cement, or position a
Band-Aid across your finger, and attach the tabs on
either side to the portrait.

**PRESENTATION**

You will probably want your children to write their
own narratives, but here are some brief monologues
for a few picture-book biographies. Use the first-person voice if you are speaking as the subject of the
biography. These monologues are written in the third
person to use with the portraits provided.

The generic-reader puppet portraits can talk
about more than one biography.

## Marie Curie

She was called Manya by her family and friends. In 1891 she was the first and only female student at the Sorbonne in Paris. When she finished her studies, she worked for and eventually married a respected scientist. She and her husband, Pierre, were awarded the Nobel Prize in physics for their work isolating radium. Several years later she was awarded another Nobel Prize in chemistry. Marie Curie was a great scientist recognized around the world. And the book is *Marie Curie* by Leonard Everett Fisher, art by the author (Macmillan, 1994).

## Cleopatra

Cleopatra was only eighteen years old when she became queen of Egypt, way back in 51 B.C.

She had to rule with her ten-year-old brother, Ptolemy. She was in love with Julius Caesar, a man thirty years older than she. When Caesar died, she married another Roman general, Mark Anthony. They attempted to rule both Egypt and Rome, engaging in sea battles and palace intrigue. Cleopatra never quite succeeded in controlling the world. She was only thirty-nine when she died, but hers was not a boring life. The book is *Cleopatra* by Diane Stanley, art by Peter Vennema (Morrow, 1994).

## Elijah McCoy

Ever hear the expression "the real McCoy"? Before the Civil War, it was illegal for African American children to learn how to read and write. Elijah McCoy, an African American, was sent to Scotland to learn to be an engineer. By the time he returned to the United States, the slaves had been freed, but he still couldn't find a very good job. He worked for the railroad as an oilman. He invented an important cup that automatically oiled machinery and in 1872 got a patent for his invention. Many manufacturers tried to imitate McCoy's invention, but people wanted the "real McCoy." And the book is *The Real McCoy: The Life of an African-American Inventor* by Wendy Towle, art by Wil Clay (Scholastic, 1993).

## Josephine Baker

"I'm gonna be a honkey-tonk dancer, and I'm gonna make lots of money." That is what Tumpie said to her stepfather. She would kick up her heels and dance barefoot up and down the sidewalks of St. Louis. She insisted on dancing on the Medicine Man's stage and earned a silver dollar. And when she grew up, she performed in a Broadway show in New York and lived in Paris, France, as the famous dancer Josephine Baker. And the book is *Ragtime Tumpie* by Alan Schroeder, art by Bernie Fuchs (Little, 1989).

## Nelson Mandela

When he was a young boy they called him Buti and he lived in a small village in South Africa. When he went to school his teacher gave him the new name of Nelson. When he moved to

Johannesburg, he worked at a law firm and went to school at night. Shocked at the treatment of the Africans, he vowed to fight for justice and equality. After spending twenty-seven years in prison, he was released, still eager to fight for what is right. He became the first black president of South Africa. And the book is *Mandela, from the Life of the South African Statesman* by Floyd Cooper, art by the author (Philomel, 1996).

## Self-Portraits

Children can draw portraits of themselves and present their own life story. See also Barnabas Kindersley and Anabel Kindersley's *Children Just like Me,* (Dorling Kindersley, 1995). Photo portraits show children from thirty countries. Each double spread tells about the country through the everyday life of a native child.

# Paper-Cup Puppets

Paper-cup puppets are terrific for a daily "book break." Every day someone, child or adult, pops into each classroom or library division with an oral "book break." Because you have alerted staff you will be coming sometime, you have not scheduled your visit and don't want to overstay your welcome. Talk briefly about a book. At the end when you are repeating the author and title of the book, push up your puppet.

# Sample Book Breaks

**YOU WILL NEED**

crayons

paper cup

paper

drinking straw

scissors

transparent tape

**PREPARATION**

Draw a character from a favorite book on paper. Cut out the picture. It should be small enough to fit into the paper cup. Affix the picture to one end of the straw with tape.

Make a hole in the bottom of the cup large enough for the straw to fit through. Your puppet will hide in the cup until you push it out to announce the book title and author to the audience.

Paper scenery can be glued behind the puppet onto the rim of the cup.

**PRESENTATION**
Plan to vary your "book breaks" by using a mix of book genres for your material for your mini-talks: fiction, informational books, biographies, poetry, and picture books.

## New Immigrants

Were you born in America? Was your mom born here? Chances are that one of your relatives was born in another country and came here as an immigrant. The first people in America were nomads who walked from Asia to what is now Alaska thousands of years ago. Many years later immigrants arrived by boat. Today, people are still arriving. They often come by airplane. Here is a new immigrant flying to America [*show puppet*]. I hope she'll be happy here. To find out more about immigration, read *Coming to America: The Story of Immigration* by Betsy Maestro, with art by Susannah Ryan (Scholastic, 1996).

## Books and Movies

Sometimes people ask me, "What is your favorite book?" Usually I answer, "the book I just finished." In this book, Moira's all-time favorite book is *Gone with the Wind*. The movie is coming to town, but her church has said that Catholics should not see it. Moira, who is Catholic, thinks that isn't fair. How can she possibly see the film? Moira plays with paper dolls representing the characters in the book and film. Maybe one looked like this [*show puppet*]. Read *The Most Wonderful Movie in the World* by Barbara Ford (Dutton, 1996).

## Honeybees

Have you ever wondered what it would be like to be a bee and live in a beehive? Now you can find out as you travel with Miss Frizzle's class in the Magic School Bus, which has turned into a beehive. Her students have all turned into honeybees. This bee is doing the waggle dance looking for food [*show puppet*]. Read *The Magic School Bus inside a Beehive* by Joanna Cole, with art by Bruce Degen (Scholastic, 1996).

## Wilma Rudolph

When Wilma was a little girl she was stricken with polio. People said she would never walk and certainly not run again. They underestimated Wilma Rudolph. She won three Olympic gold medals for her running. These are her medals [*show medals*]. Read *Wilma Unlimited* by Kathleen Krull, with art by David Diaz (Harcourt, 1996).

# Ducks in the City

Tokyo is a big, big city in Japan. Living in Tokyo are almost 12 million people—plus, in this true story, a family of ducks. The city people are thrilled to have wild ducks nesting in the city park. There is even a "duck watch" on the nightly television news. Chibi, the youngest duckling, is everyone's favorite, but then he is lost in a typhoon. Will he be found? Here is Chibi in a picture taken by Mr. Sato [*show picture*]. Read *Chibi: A True Story from Japan* by Barbara Brenner and Julia Takaya, with art by June Otani (Clarion, 1996).

# Stick Puppets

$S$tick puppets are the easiest of all to make and use. They are simply pictures with handles.

**YOU WILL NEED**
crayons
poster paper
cellophane tape
3 x 5 index cards
paint stirrers or dowels

**PREPARATION**
To make the stick puppets for the plays that follow, enlarge the patterns. The easiest way to do so is on a duplicating machine with an enlargement feature. If the machine in your building doesn't have one, go to your local commercial copy center. You can use just the front side of the pattern or you can enlarge the back patterns for the figures, too. If you don't wish to use the patterns, draw a character, an object, or scene on poster paper and color.

For one-dimensional puppets, on the back of the picture, tape an index card on the top and two sides to create a pocket for the handle. For padded puppets, fasten the two pattern sides together with staples, leaving enough room on the bottom to stuff the puppets and insert the stick/handle. Use wadded tissue paper to pad the shape and give it a three-dimensional look.

## PRESENTATION

Donkeys have long been used throughout the world to carry bundles and people. Donkey stories told as jokes are popular in the Middle East. There are also a number of talks featuring this stubborn but useful animal that are told in Latin America. The German story of the trickster Tyll Ulenspeigel teaching a donkey to read is similar to the Middle Eastern *Mustafa's Brilliant Donkey,* offered here. The following stories are all set in a fantasy Middle East, so you can use the same puppets for all the skits.

Tell these stories with a puppeteer narrator and padded stick puppets. The padded puppets, filled with paper to give them shape, are an optional method. Once you or your children have made a set of these puppets, they can be used to tell several donkey stories, one after the other, in a theme program or one at a time when you want to "put on a play."

# Donkey Plays

The following skits have been scripted, but the jokes can be told in narrative form, too, while the appropriate puppets are activated.

## Selling Lemons

**CHARACTERS**

| | |
|---|---|
| Mustafa | Buyer 1 |
| Donkey, with Velcro strip | Buyer 2 |

**PROPS**

basket of lemons, with Velcro strip

MUSTAFA: I am so happy. Today is market day. I have a basket filled with lemons from the tree in my yard. I am sure to sell them all. My donkey will carry the basket to market for me. Here, donkey.

[Donkey *comes onstage with a basket of lemons attached with Velcro.*]

DONKEY: Hee-haw, hee-haw.

MUSTAFA: [*Laughing*]: You sound as though you are advertising my lemons.

DONKEY: Hee-haw, hee-haw. [Mustafa *and* donkey *walk back and forth across stage.*]

MUSTAFA: Here we are at the market. Now I can sell my lemons. Lemons, lemons.

DONKEY: Hee-haw, hee-haw.

MUSTAFA: Quiet, donkey. No one will buy my lemons if you keep making a racket.

DONKEY: Hee-haw, hee-haw.

MUSTAFA: Lemons . . . Lemons . . . Lemons . . .

DONKEY: Hee-haw, hee-haw.

BUYER 1: Look at Mustafa trying to sell his lemons. What a noise his donkey is making.

BUYER 2: Look—a crowd is gathering. The donkey seems to be in competition with Mustafa.

MUSTAFA: Lemons . . . Lemons . . . Lemons . . .

DONKEY: Hee-haw . . . hee-haw . . .

MUSTAFA: Quiet, donkey. Who is selling these lemons? Me or you?

BUYER 1: I'll buy a lemon, Mustafa.

BUYER 2: [*Laughing*]: I'll buy two lemons. Do I give the money to you or to your donkey?

BUYER 1: You should pay your donkey for selling your lemons. I'll buy two more.

MUSTAFA: I have sold all my lemons. Donkey, I'm sorry that I scolded you. It turns out that you are a better salesman than me. Thank you.

DONKEY: Hee-haw, hee-haw.

# A Rial for a Donkey

**CHARACTERS**

Mustafa

Donkey, with Velcro strip

Friend 1

Friend 2

Cat, with Velcro strip

DONKEY: Hee-haw, hee-haw.

MUSTAFA: Miserable donkey. Walk faster. We can't take all day to bring these lemons to market.

FRIEND 1: Mustafa, I thought you loved your donkey.

MUSTAFA: It is true that in the past I have said that I love my donkey, but today he is being as stubborn as a, as a . . . donkey. I would sell him to anyone for a single rial.

FRIEND 2: I'll buy your donkey for a rial.

FRIEND 1: I'll buy your donkey for a rial.

MUSTAFA: [*To himself*]: What have I done? I do love my miserable donkey. I can't sell him for one rial. He is worth much, much more. I can't go back on my word. I will sell my donkey for one rial, but not here. I will sell him at the market.

DONKEY: Hee-haw, hee-haw.

MUSTAFA: [*Alone onstage*]: What shall I do? I don't want to sell my donkey for one rial. I don't want to sell him for any amount of money.

[Mustafa *leaves stage. Two friends reappear.*]

FRIEND 1: Poor Mustafa. Today is market day. He promised to sell his donkey for one rial. I know he didn't mean it.

FRIEND 2: If he doesn't want to sell his donkey, Mustafa should not have said he would sell him for so little money.

[Mustafa *and* donkey *return to stage.* Donkey *has* cat *on his back, attached with Velcro.*]

DONKEY:  Hee-haw, hee-haw.

FRIEND 1:  Hello, Mustafa's donkey. Are you ready to go home with me?

FRIEND 2:  You don't want to go home with him. I'm going to buy you for one rial.

CAT:  [Cat's *meow can be made by any player, or the audience can help here.*] Meow, meow, meow.

MUSTAFA:  Yes. Today is the day that I am selling my donkey for one rial, but as you know my donkey can not be parted from his friend the cat.

DONKEY:  Hee-haw, hee-haw.

CAT:  Meow, meow, meow.

MUSTAFA:  The cost of the cat is 500 rials. The cost of the donkey remains the same: one rial. The two together are 500 and one rials.

FRIEND 1:  Mustafa is clever. Now he won't have to sell his donkey.

FRIEND 2:  Odd. I've never seen that cat before.

DONKEY:  Hee-haw, hee-haw.

CAT:  Meow, meow, meow.

# My Donkey, Your Donkey

**CHARACTERS**

| | |
|---|---|
| Mustafa | White donkey |
| Friend | Black donkey |

MUSTAFA: I can never tell my donkey from your donkey.

FRIEND: Just remember one thing about my donkey that is different from your donkey, and you will always be able to tell the difference.

MUSTAFA: That's a good idea. I will cut a few hairs from my donkey's tail. Then my donkey's tail will be shorter than your donkey's tail. [Mustafa *leaves stage and returns.*]

FRIEND: Now can you tell your donkey from my donkey?

MUSTAFA: No. Unfortunately, your donkey's tail got caught in a bush. He lost a few hairs; the tails are the same length.

FRIEND: Why don't you put a little nick in your donkey's ear? Your donkey's ear will be different from my donkey's ear.

MUSTAFA: Good idea. I will do it right now. [Mustafa *leaves stage and returns.*]

FRIEND: Now can you tell my donkey from your donkey?

MUSTAFA: No. Unfortunately, your donkey caught his ear in the fence. The ears of your donkey and my donkey are the same.

FRIEND: Have you ever noticed that your donkey is taller than my donkey?

MUSTAFA: Thank you, my friend. Now I will always be able to tell your *white* donkey from my *black* donkey. [*Bring* white and black donkeys *to stage so audience can "see" punch line.*]

DONKEYS: Hee-haw, hee-haw.

## Donkey for Sale

**CHARACTERS**

| | |
|---|---|
| Mustafa | Buyer 1 |
| Donkey | Buyer 2 |

MUSTAFA: You miserable donkey. I am going to take you to market and sell you.

DONKEY: Hee-haw, hee-haw.

BUYER 1: Here comes Mustafa with his donkey.

BUYER 2: He is always threatening to sell him.

MUSTAFA: What am I bid for this beautiful donkey? Notice his handsome head.

BUYER 1: The donkey does have a nice head.

MUSTAFA: What am I bid for this beautiful donkey? Look at his strong legs.

BUYER 2: The donkey does seem to have strong legs.

MUSTAFA: What am I bid for this beautiful donkey? Please note his shiny coat.

BUYER 1: The donkey does have a shiny coat.

MUSTAFA: What am I bid for this beautiful donkey? Listen to his lovely voice.

DONKEY: Hee-haw, hee-haw.

BUYER 1: The donkey does have a melodic voice.

BUYER 2: I'll give you five rials for your donkey.

BUYER 1: I'll give you ten.

BUYER 2: I'll give you fifteen.

MUSTAFA: I'll give you twenty.

BUYER 1: Mustafa, you are bidding on your own donkey.

MUSTAFA: Yes, you are right. After telling you both how wonderful my donkey is, I've decided not to sell him. Come miserable donkey, we are going home.

DONKEY: Hee-haw, hee-haw.

# Mustafa's Brilliant Donkey

## CHARACTERS

Mustafa　　　　Friend 1

Donkey　　　　Friend 2

## PROP
book on stand

## Scene 1

MUSTAFA: My donkey is brilliant. He is the smartest donkey in the whole world.

FRIEND 1: Donkeys are never smart.

MUSTAFA: My donkey is clever.

FRIEND 2: In what way is he clever?

MUSTAFA: I can teach this donkey to read.

FRIEND 1: Animals don't read.

FRIEND 2: Donkeys can't be taught to read.

MUSTAFA: I will show you that my donkey can be taught to read. Meet me here in a month.

FRIEND 1: We will meet you here, but I doubt that you can teach your donkey to read.

[*All exit.*]

## Scene 2

FRIEND 2: Here comes Mustafa with his donkey.

FRIEND 1: I wonder if he really taught his donkey to read.

[*Place reading stand with book onstage.*]

MUSTAFA: Here we are. My clever donkey and I are ready to show you what he has learned so far in his reading.

DONKEY: [*with nose to book*]: Hee-haw, hee-haw.

MUSTAFA: See. He already knows two sounds in the alphabet.

FRIEND 1: Mustafa is as clever as a . . . , clever as a . . . donkey.

DONKEY: Hee-haw, hee-haw.


## Clever Donkey or Clever Mustafa?

**CHARACTERS**
Friend
Mustafa
Donkey

**PROP**
rope with bell to place on donkey's neck (A Christmas-package bell can be used instead of the paper pattern provided.)

FRIEND: Thank you, Mustafa, for inviting me to tea, but how can you stay inside and still earn a living?

MUSTAFA: My donkey is working for me.

FRIEND: What do you mean?

MUSTAFA: I own a well. My donkey walks around the well and hauls up buckets of water.

FRIEND: How do you know that he is working with no one watching him?

MUSTAFA: I can hear the bell tied around his neck.

FRIEND: But what if the donkey is standing still and just shaking his head from side to side so that you think that he is working?

MUSTAFA: If my donkey were that clever, he would be in here drinking tea, and I would be out there by the well working for him.

[*Place* donkey *wearing bell onstage.*]


## Books to Share: Donkeys

Brittain, Bill. *Devil's Donkey*. Art by Andrew Glass. Harper, 1981. Short novel to share aloud. Dan'l Pitt doesn't believe Old Magda, the witch, but she can and does turn him into a donkey.

Grimm, Jacob. *The Donkey Prince*. Art by Barbara Cooney. Adapted by M. Jean Craig. Doubleday, 1977. The donkey child will stay in animal shape until someone loves him as he is.

Milne, A. A. *Winnie the Pooh*. Art by Ernest H. Shepard. Dutton, 1988. This childhood classic features lively read-aloud chapters about the animals, including Eeyore, the old gray donkey.

Steig, William. *Sylvester and the Magic Pebble*. Art by the author. Simon, 1988. Sylvester the donkey is excited about the wishing pebble that he found, until he wishes that he were a rock!

# Caribbean Capers

I first read this story in a book by Pura Belpré published in 1932. The Puerto Rican tale is told to Spanish-speaking children throughout the Caribbean. Elida Bonet, a librarian in Texas, remembered the story from her childhood in Panama and sent me a version of it.

My husband, Peter, and I have been struggling to learn Spanish since we moved to Florida. The names of animals and food mentioned in the story are perfect for beginning and intermediate Spanish students. I've adapted the story from the versions that I have heard.

When I tell the story, I worry that children will be sad with the death of Raton Perez, but so far everyone has ignored the death and has been entranced with the cockroach and her ribbons.

Although this has been scripted, don't feel that your puppeteers need to stick to the written word. It may be used in the same way that you prepare a story for creative dramatization. Read the script as a story; assign parts; let the children make up their own dialogue. Add, delete, or change the animals depending on what you have in your puppet collection.

Encourage audience participation. Inform the audience members that they will help tell the story using animal sounds, then cue them at the appropriate time.

**CHARACTERS**

Narrator (a puppet, a voice only, or a person standing in front of the stage; I prefer a person, who can also assist the puppets if they need help with props)

Carolina Cucharacha, a cockroach

Señor Toro, a bull          Señor Gallo, a rooster

Señor Rana, a frog          Señor Perro, a dog

Señor Pato, a duck          Señor Raton Perez, a rat

Señor Cerdo, a pig

**PROPS**

| | | |
|---|---|---|
| coin | ribbons | pot |
| mirror | wedding veil | stool |

## Carolina Cucharacha and the Golden Coin

NARRATOR: There was once a roach named Carolina. Most people don't think cockroaches are pretty, but Carolina was beautiful. She dressed festively, too. She always wore petticoats, ribbons in her hair, and elegant earrings.

She was popular with the men, but picky about whom she would marry. On a bright, sunny day, Carolina was scurrying home when she found a gold coin on the path to her house.

CAROLINA: I am rich! Now I can buy anything I want. But what do I want?

Should I buy eggs? No. If I buy eggs, they will probably break before I get them home.

Should I buy chocolate? No. Chocolate would make me fat.

Should I buy strawberries? No. Strawberries will spoil before I want to eat them.

Should I buy bread? No. I can make my own bread.

What should I buy?

Should I buy fish? No. It's too much trouble to cook.

Should I buy meat? No. I have enough meat.

NARRATOR: Carolina Cucharacha looked in the mirror.

CAROLINA: [*admiring herself in mirror*] I will buy ribbons. Ribbons for my hair. Ribbons for my neck. Ribbons for my dress, ribbons for my shoes. Ribbons, ribbons, ribbons.

[Carolina *puts on ribbons.*]

NARRATOR: If Carolina was beautiful before, now she was stunningly delicious.

All the animals wanted to marry her. Señor Toro, the bull, came courting. Carolina Cucharacha sat in her rocking chair bedecked in ribbons.

TORO: Will you marry me, Señorita Carolina?

CAROLINA: What do you say when you greet the day?

TORO: Moo. Moo. Moo.

CAROLINA: No, thank you. I will not marry you.

NARRATOR: Señor Rana, the frog, came courting. Carolina Cucharacha sat in her rocking chair bedecked in ribbons.

RANA: Will you marry me, Señorita Carolina?

CAROLINA: What do you say when you greet the day?

RANA: Croak. Croak. Croak.

CAROLINA: No, thank you. I will not marry you.

NARRATOR: Señor Pato, the duck, came courting. Carolina Cucharacha sat in her rocking chair bedecked in ribbons.

PATO: Will you marry me, Señorita Carolina?

CAROLINA: What do you say when you greet the day?

PATO: Quack. Quack. Quack.

CAROLINA: No, thank you. I will not marry you.

NARRATOR: Señor Cerdo, the pig, came courting. Carolina Cucharacha sat in her rocking chair bedecked in ribbons.

CERDO: Will you marry me, Señorita Carolina?

CAROLINA: What do you say when you greet the day?

CERDO: Oink. Oink. Oink.

CAROLINA: No, thank you. I will not marry you.

NARRATOR: Señor Gallo, the rooster, came courting. Carolina Cucharacha sat in her rocking chair bedecked in ribbons.

GALLO: Will you marry me, Señorita Carolina?

CAROLINA: What do you say when you greet the day?

GALLO: Cock-a-doodle-doo. Cock-a-doodle-doo. Cock-a-doodle-doo.

CAROLINA: No, thank you. I will not marry you.

NARRATOR: Señor Perro, the dog, came courting. Carolina Cucharacha sat in her rocking chair bedecked in ribbons.

PERRO: Will you marry me, Señorita Carolina?

CAROLINA: What do you say when you greet the day?

PERRO: Woof. Woof. Woof.

CAROLINA: No, thank you. I will not marry you.

NARRATOR: Señor Raton Perez, the rat, came courting. Carolina Cucharacha sat in her rocking chair bedecked in ribbons.

RATON: Will you marry me, Señorita Carolina?

CAROLINA: What do you say when you greet the day?

RATON: Chuc. Chuc. Chuc.

CAROLINA: How charming. Of course, I'll marry you.

NARRATOR: The wedding was elegant. There was dancing and singing. Señor Toro gave a toast.

TORO: Moo. Moo. Moo.

NARRATOR: Señor Rana gave a toast.

RANA: Croak. Croak. Croak.

NARRATOR: Señor Pato gave a toast.

PATO: Quack. Quack. Quack.

NARRATOR: Señor Cerdo gave a toast.

CERDO: Oink. Oink. Oink.

NARRATOR: Señor Perro gave a toast.

PERRO: Woof. Woof. Woof.

NARRATOR: Señor Gallo gave a toast.

GALLO: Cock-a-doodle-doo. Cock-a-doodle-doo. Cock-a-doodle-doo.

NARRATOR: Señor Raton Perez and Señora Carolina were happy. But Señor Raton Perez was a glutton. He always wanted to eat. Señora Carolina spent many hours in the kitchen cooking. One day she made a stew. She put meat and vegetables into a big pot and put it on the stove to simmer.

CAROLINA: Husband, I am going out to the market. Don't go near the boiling pot in the kitchen. It is very hot. We will have dinner when I return.

NARRATOR: Señor Raton Perez the glutton did not heed his wife's advice. As soon as she had closed the door, he ran into the kitchen. He pulled a stool over to the stove, climbed up, and looked into the pot, smelling the delicious aroma of the stew. Greedy Raton Perez. He leaned farther and farther into the pot until—whoops! He fell into the pot. [Raton Perez *falls into pot or simply falls in back of stage.*] That was the end of Raton Perez.

ALL: [*Crying sounds*]

NARRATOR: Was Carolina Cucharacha sad? I think so; after all, she loved his soft "Chuc. Chuc. Chuc." Now Carolina sits on the porch in her rocking chair wearing her beautiful clothes and singing.

CAROLINA: I found a coin.

I married a rat.

He loved to eat

And that is that.

NARRATOR: The animals come to pay their respects to the lovely cockroach Carolina Cucharacha.

[*Animals return to stage, make their animal sounds, and take a bow.*]

The end.

## La Historia de Cucaracha Carolina

*Translated by José Danschin*

NARRADOR: Había una vez una cucaracha llamada Carolina. Mucha gente no piensa que las cucarachas son lindas, Pero Carolina era hermosa. A demás ella se vestía festiva. Ella siempre usaba chalecos, cintas en su cabello, y aretes elegantes. Ella era popular con los hombres, pero selectiva con quien ella se casaría. En un brillante día soleado, Carolina estaba corriendo apresurada a su casa, cuando en el camino, ella se encontró una moneda de oro.

CAROLINA: !Soy rica! Ahora me puedo comprar cualquier cosa, lo que yo quiera. Pero, ¿Qué es lo que quiero? ¿Debería yo comprar huevos? No, si yo compro huevos provablemente se romperían antes que lleguen a casa. ¿Debería comprarme chocolate? No, el chocolate me engordaría.

¿Debería comprarme fresas? No, las fresas se danarían antes de comermelos.

¿Debería yo comprar pan? No, yo puedo hacer mi propio pan.

¿Entonces qué debería comprar?

¿Debería comprar pescado? No, cocinarlo es mucho problema.

¿Debería comprar carne? No, tengo suficiente carne.

NARRADOR: Carolina cucaracha se miró en el espejo.

[Carolina *se admira ella misma en el espejo.*]

CAROLINA: Me compraré cintas. Cintas para mi cabello. Cintas para mi cuello. Cintas para mi vestido. Cintas para mis zapatos. Cintas. Cintas. Cintas.

[Carolina *se pone cintas.*]

NARRADOR: Si antes Carolina era hermosa, ahora ella estaba estupendamente sabrosa. Todos los animales quisieron casarse con ella.

Señor Toro, el toro vino a cortejarla. Cucaracha Carolina se sentó en su mecedora adornada en cintas.

TORO: ¿Se casaría conmigo, Señorita Carolina?

CAROLINA: ¿Qué es lo que usted dice cuando saluda al día?

TORO: Muu. Muu. Muu.

CAROLINA: No gracias. Yo no me casaría contigo.

NARRADOR: Señor Rana, el sapo vino a cortejarla. Cucaracha Carolina se sentó en su mecedora adornada en cintas.

RANA: ¿Se casaría conmigo, Señorita Carolina?

CAROLINA: ¿Qué es lo que usted dice cuando saluda al día?

RANA: Croak. Croak. Croak.

CAROLINA: No gracias. Yo no me casaría contigo.

NARRADOR: Señor Pato, el pato vino a cortejarla. Cucaracha Carolina se sentó en su mecedora adornada en cintas.

PATO: ¿Se casaría conmigo, Señorita Carolina?

CAROLINA: ¿Qué es lo que usted dice cuando saluda al día?

PATO: Cuac. Cuac. Cuac.

CAROLINA: No gracias. Yo no me casaría contigo.

NARRADOR: Señor Cerdo, el cerdo vino a cortejarla. Cucaracha Carolina se sentó en su mecedora adornada en cintas.

CERDO: ¿Se casaría conmigo, Señorita Carolina?

CAROLINA: ¿Qué es lo que usted dice cuando saluda al dia?

CERDO: Oink. Oink. Oink.

CAROLINA: No gracias. Yo no me casaría contigo.

NARRADOR: Señor Gallo, el gallo vino a cortejarla.

Cucaracha Carolina se sentó en su mecedora adornada en cintas.

GALLO: Se casaría conmigo, Señorita Carolina?

CAROLINA: ¿Que es lo que usted dice cuando saluda al día?

GALLO: Kikiriki. Kikiriki. Kikiriki.

CAROLINA: No gracias. Yo no me casaría contigo.

NARRADOR: Señor Perro, el perro, vino a cortejarla. Cucaracha Carolina se sentó en su mecedora adornada en cintas.

PERRO: ¿Se casaría conmigo, Señorita Carolina?

CAROLINA: ¿Qué es lo que usted dice cuando saluda al día?

PERRO: Guau. Guau. Guau.

CAROLINA: No gracias. Yo no me casaría contigo.

NARRADOR: Señor Ratón Perez, el ratón, vino a cortejarla. Cucaracha Carolina se sentó en su mecedora adornada en cintas.

RATÓN: ¿Se casaría conmigo, Señorita Carolina?

CAROLINA: ¿Que es lo que usted dice cuando saluda al día?

RATÓN: Cuis. Cuis. Cuis.

CAROLINA: ¡Qué encantador! Claro que sí, yo me casaría contigo.

NARRADOR: La boda fue elegante. Bailaron y cantaron. El Señor Toro dió un brindis.

TORO: Muu. Muu. Muu.

NARRADOR: El Señor Rana dió un brindis.

RANA: Croak. Croak. Croak.

NARRADOR: El Señor Pato dió un brindis.

PATO: Cuac. Cuac. Cuac.

NARRADOR: El señor Cerdo dió un brindis.

CERDO: Oink, Oink, Oink.

NARRADOR: El Señor Perro dió un brindis.

PERRO: Guau. Guau. Guau.

NARRADOR: El Señor Gallo dió un brindis.

GALLO: Kikiriki. Kikiriki. Kikiriki.

NARRADOR: El Señor Ratón Perez y la Señora Carolina fueron felices. Pero el Señor Ratón era un glotón. Él siempre quería comer. La Señora Carolina pasaba muchas horas en la concina cocinando. Un día ella hizo un guisado. Ella puso carne y vegetales en unal olla grande, y lo puso en la estufa para que se concinara a fuego lento.

CAROLINA: Esposo, estoy yendo al mercado. No te acerques a la olla hirviendo que esta en la cocina. Está muy caliente. Comeremos a mi regreso.

NARRADOR: El Señor Ratón Perez el glotón no hizo caso de los consejos de su esposa. Tan pronto ella se asomó a la puerta, él corrió para la cocina. Él jaló un taburete encima de la estufa, se subió y miró dentro la olla que olía un aroma delicioso del guisado. Codicioso Ratón Perez. Se inclinó adelante y adelante a la olla hasta que: ¡Upss! Él se cayó en la olla. [Ratón Perez *se cayó en la olla, o simplemente se cayó detrás del escenario.*] Ese fue el fin de Ratón Perez.

TODOS: [*Sonidos de llanto, fingir llorando.*]

NARRADOR: ¿Carolina Cucaracha estaba triste? Yo pienso que sí, despues de todo ella amaba su tierno "Cuis. Cuis. Cuis." Ahora Carolina se sienta en el pórtico, en su mecedora vistiendo sus trajes hermosos y cantando.

CAROLINA: Me encontré una moneda.

Me casé con un Ratón.

A él le gustaba comer.

Y eso es eso.

NARRADOR: Los animales vinieron a ofrecer sus respetos a la adorable Cucaracha Carolina.

[*Los animales regresan al escenario haciendo sus sonidos respectivos de animales y hacen una reverencia.*]

El final.


Let your Carolina Cucharacha puppet recite these two cockroach poems.

## The History of the Cockroach

*Rick Walton*

A million gazillion years ago
the first cockroach hatched and said, "Hello!"

"Hello there," it said to the rocks and the trees.
"Hello" to the fishes that crept from the seas.

"Hello" to the dinosaurs stomping the ground.
"Hello!" to the people when they came around.

And someday when all of us finally die,
the cockroach will be there to tell us, "Good-bye!"

And after it sheds a few small cockroach tears,
it will live for a million gazillion more years.

## Cockroach Sandwich

*Colin McNaughton*

Cockroach sandwich
For my lunch,
Hate the taste
But love the crunch!

See also "Cockroach" by Yoshido Uchida in
*Presenting Reader's Theater* by Caroline Feller Bauer,
art by Lynn Bredeson (Wilson, 1987).

## Books to Share

BUGS

Fleischman, Paul. *Joyful Noise: Poems for Two Voices.* Art by Eric Beddows. Harper, 1988. Insects are playfully described in two voices.

James, Mary. *Shoebag.* Scholastic, 1990. A cockroach is turned into a boy. See also *Shoebag Returns* (Scholastic, 1996).

Walton, Rick. *What to Do When a Bug Climbs in Your Mouth and Other Poems to Drive You Buggy.* Art by Nancy Carlson. Lothrop, 1995. Cartoon drawings large enough to share accompany the buggy poems.

CARIBBEAN

Agard, John, and Grace Nichols, eds. *A Caribbean Dozen: Poems from Caribbean Poets.* Art by Cathie Felstead. Candlewick, 1990. Thirteen Caribbean poets from Trinidad, Jamaica, and Guyana are represented in this collection.

Bloom, Valerie. *Fruits: A Caribbean Counting Poem.* Art by David Axtel. Holt, 1997. In Jamaican Patwa, two little girls count fruits of the Caribbean.

Gunning, Monica. *Not a Copper Penny in Me House: Poems from the Caribbean.* Art by Frané Lessac. Boyds Mills, 1993. These short poems and bright pictures highlight the essence of Caribbean villages.

Hallworth, Grace. *Down by the River: Afro-Caribbean Rhymes, Games, and Songs for Children.* Art by

Caroline Binch. Scholastic, 1996. Picture-book collection of rhymes and chants.

Jekyll, Walter. *I Have a News: Rhymes from the Caribbean*. Art by Jacqueline Mair. Lothrop, 1994. Rhythmic rhymes, music included.

Joseph, Lynn. *A Wave in Her Pocket: Stories from Trinidad*. Art by Brian Pinkney. Clarion, 1991. Traditional stories told by "tantie."

Williams, Karen Lynn. *Tap-Tap*. Art by Catherine Stock. Clarion, 1994. In a Haitian market, Sasifi earns a surprise.

# Feet Puppets
## *Walks*

This is a silly idea and lots of fun to try.

**YOU WILL NEED**
white socks
felt-tip marker or felt and yarn

**PREPARATION**
Clothe your two feet in white socks. Draw faces on the soles of white socks with a felt-tip marker. Drawing will be easier if you slip a piece of poster board into the sock to create a solid surface.

**PRESENTATION**
You will probably want to perform with your feet puppets only briefly.

One way to enjoy this idea is to lie on your back on the floor facing a floor-to-ceiling mirror. You give the feet puppet show to yourself. When you want to perform for an audience, you can lie on the floor with your feet facing the audience, or the performers can lie on a table showing their puppet feet.

Played enough with feet puppets? Now take the socks off your (squeaky-clean) feet and use the same puppets as hand puppets.

## What Feet Puppets Can Do

The two puppets can

> discuss a walk or hike
>
> sway to a taped musical selection
>
> talk about books they have read that feature walks

### Books to Share: Walks

Barasch, Lynne. *A Winter Walk*. Art by the author. Houghton, 1993. A little girl and her mother enjoy a walk in the winter fields.

deRegniers, Beatrice Schenk. *Going for a Walk*. Art by Robert Knox. Harper, 1993. A little girl greets animals and a little boy as she takes a walk.

Hindley, Judy. *Funny Walks*. Art by Alex Ayliffe. Bridgewater, 1994. In rhymed text, the reader is introduced to different ways animals and people walk.

Ryder, Joanne. *The Goodbye Walk*. Art by Deborah Haeffele. Lodestar, 1993. A young girl says good-bye to her favorite vacation places.

# Simple
# String Puppets

These string puppets are easy-to-make-and-use marionettes. They require only one or—if you want to be a bit more sophisticated—two strings. The strings have little chance of becoming tangled, but the puppet moves freely.

**YOU WILL NEED**

crayons                          3 x 5 index cards
paper                            tape
scissors                         paint sticks or dowels
string or yarn

**PREPARATION**

All the ants in the story can be reproduced from the drawings provided, or you can make your own designs, giving individual personalities to each ant. Mom and Baby Ant are stick puppets. Attach paint sticks or dowels to each puppet by taping an index card to the back of the drawing. Leave the bottom of the card open to hold the stick.

The dancing ants in this story can also be reproduced from the pattern, or children can design their

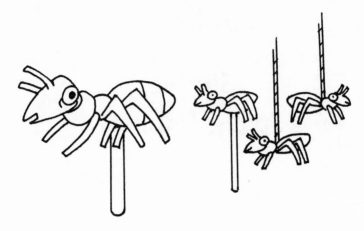

own. Attach yarn or string to the center of the back of each ant with tape. If you construct giant ants, you may want to attach two strings, one at either end of the ant for better balance.

The stage is a table. The setting is a picnic table, so place real food on the stage table, your own lunch perhaps, or use cardboard cutouts on stands to represent the food.

### PRESENTATION
The performers holding the stick puppets stand or kneel behind the stage while they speak the lines of the play.

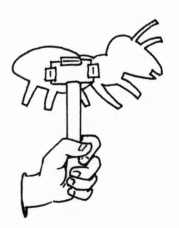

The string-puppet performers hold the string and dangle the ants to make them dance.

### CHARACTERS
Mom Ant

Baby Ant

Dancing ants, as many as you want

**PROPS**

real or cardboard food

music, live or recorded, for dancing ants (optional); see Lorna Philbot and Graham Philpot, *Amazing Anthony Ant*, p. 115, for song material.

# Picnic Story; or
# Why Ants Have Small Waists

MOM ANT: This picnic is a real feast.

BABY ANT: Look at the chocolate cake, the potato chips, even jelly-and-peanut-butter sandwiches. I can't wait to sample them all.

MOM ANT: Eat as much as you want, but don't let the people see you. Remember that our job is to bring as much back to the Home Hill as we can.

BABY ANT: The people are eating almost everything, but they already seem so fat.

MOM ANT: We are lucky. We never get too fat. We always have lovely slim waists. While you enjoy the cake, I'll tell you why: Many, many years ago in China, there lived an emperor with a pretty but frail daughter. He wanted to please her. He asked her, "What do you want, my child?"

BABY ANT: [*in Princess's voice*] I love the color of gold. I would like to have a new gold necklace and a gold bracelet to match.

MOM ANT: The Emperor thought and thought; how could he find enough gold to make new jewelry for the Princess?

BABY ANT: He thought of *Ants!*

MOM ANT: Right. He knew what good workers we are. He asked us to go down to the bottom of the sea and the deep canyons to find gold. Each ant tied a silk thread around its waist, and we were lowered to the bottom of the sea and down all the deep canyons.

[Dancing ants *appear above table and dance and sing. Mom and Baby can leave stage while ants sing and dance. They sing* "The Ants go Marching." Mom *and* Baby *reappear.*]

MOM ANT: The Emperor's ants were able to mine enough gold to make sparkling jewelry for the Princess, who lived to a merry old age.

BABY ANT: And because of the threads around our waists as we were lowered to the goldfields under the sea and in the deep canyons, our waists are always tiny.

DANCING ANTS and MOM ANT and BABY ANT: Let's have more chocolate cake.

[*Curtain closes on the entire cast singing* "The Ants Go Marching."]

# Ant Facts

A narrator can use these facts to introduce the sub-ject of ants, or the performing ants can each give a fact as part of an introduction or epilogue to the play.

Ants are insects.

They have six legs and two antennae
or feelers.

There are many kinds of ants.

They have been on the earth for
thousands of years.

Ants live together in an organized colony.

Each ant has a particular job to perform.

There are worker ants who carry food
back to the colony.

Some ants take care of the eggs and
the young.

Some ants dig rooms and tunnels.

The biggest and most important ant is
the queen. It is her job to lay eggs.

Ants come in several colors. They can
be black, brown, or red.

Some ants eat other insects.

Some ants eat plants.

Some ants eat caterpillars.

And it seems as though all ants like
what we eat!

~~~~~~~~~~~~~~~~~~~~~~~~~~~~~~~~~~~~~~~~~~~~~~~~~~~~~~~~~~~~

## The Ants

*Douglas Florian*

Ants are scantily
Half an inch long,
But for their size
They're very strong.
Ants tote leaves
Five times their weight
Back to their nest
At speedy rate.
They walk on tree limbs
Upside down
A hundred feet
Above the ground,
While down below
Beneath a mound
They're building tunnels
Underground.
And so it's been—
And it will be—
Since greatest
Ant antiquity.

**Books to Share: Ants**

Allinson, Beverly. *Effie.* Art by Barbara Reid. Scholastic, 1990. Effie the ant makes friends with an elephant.

Demuth, Patricia Brennan. *Those Amazing Ants.* Art by S. D. Schindler. Macmillan, 1994. Ant information in picture-book form.

Hawcock, David, and Lee Montgomery. *Ant.* Random, 1994. Information plus a spectacular three-dimensional ant.

Hepworth, Kathi. *Antics! An Alphabetical Anthology.* Putnam, 1992. Each letter of the alphabet is represented with a word containing "ant."

Jackson, Ellen. *Ants Can't Dance.* Art by Frank Remkiewicz. Macmillan, 1991. No one believes that Jonathan's pet ant talks to him.

Levitt, Paul M., Douglas A. Burger, and Elissa S. Guralnick. "E." In *The Weighty Word Book.* Manuscripts, 1985. The word "expedient" is explained with the story of a commander ant.

Philpot, Lorna, and Graham Philpot. *Amazing Anthony Ant.* Random, 1994. The song "The Ants Go Marching," illustrated with pop-up flaps.

Pinczes, Elinor J. *One Hundred Hungry Ants.* Art by Bonnie Mackain. Houghton, 1993. The principles of division are explained through an ant's picnic.

Retan, Walter. *Armies of Ants.* Art by Jean Cassels. Scholastic, 1994. Beginning readers will learn about the habits of ants.

Van Allsburg, Chris. *Two Bad Ants.* Art by the author. Houghton, 1988. On a mission to collect sugar crystals, two ants explore the kitchen.

# Cereal Box Theater
# with String Puppets

**O**n a flight from Miami to New York, we were served cereal in little individual-serving boxes. When the woman next to me saw me put the empty box into my tote bag, she asked me what I was going to do with an empty box. I was surprised. If you do something weird on an airplane, people usually just stare, but don't say anything. I took the box out of my tote and showed her my individual puppet box theater. The woman turned out to be on her way to Battle Creek, Michigan, where she worked at the headquarters of the manufacturer of the cereal that went into the box.

**YOU WILL NEED**

empty individual-serving cereal box (these small boxes should be easy to obtain: simply put a notice on the bulletin board at your school or library calling for empty individual-serving cereal boxes)

scissors

contact paper or poster paint (optional)

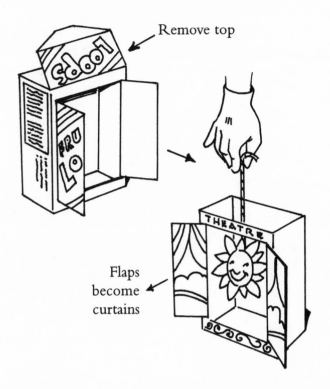

Remove top

Flaps become curtains

**PREPARATION**

For this quickly made theater, open the box from the front along the perforated lines printed by the manufacturer. The flaps create the curtain for the stage. Cut off the flaps at the top of the box. The puppeteer operates the puppets from the top opening.

Make your puppets out of fabric or paper and use yarn or a thread to dangle the puppets onto the stage. If the thread is the same color as the backdrop, it will be invisible to the audience—which, in this case, may be the same as the maker of the puppets and little theater.

A larger version can be made from a full-size cereal box. If you are working with a large group, use the larger box to provide a clear demonstration of how to make a theater with a smaller box.

### Hint

To make a more professional-looking theater, decorate the box by covering it with contact paper or painting it with poster paints.

## PRESENTATION

Paper puppets dangling from string appear to be dancing. Turn on some music and let your puppets dance to the rhythm. You can also use the puppets to underscore the rhythms and content of a recited poem. Here are two poems that work magically with paper flowers manipulated with strings.

## Flower-Ballerinas

*Barbara Juster Esbensen*

Suspended
from a fragile
strand
they're set in motion
by the breeze

Beneath
this puppet master's
hand
they dance in ruffles
twos and threes

These ballerinas
lightly
pose
with every arm
a petaled arc

They twirl and
turn on pointed
toes
each jeweled shoe
a fuchsia spark

## The Dancers

*Charlotte Zolotow*

The long yellow branches
of forsythia
and the white arms of spirea
move together
and then apart
in the light spring wind
like dancers
swaying, dipping,
to the sunlit music
of the air.

### Books to Share: Dance

For books about flowers, see "Books to Share: Gardens," page 25.

Isadora, Rachel. *Max*. Art by the author. Macmillan, 1976. Max discovers that a ballet class can help him improve his baseball skills.

Jonas, Ann. *Color Dance*. Art by the author. Greenwillow, 1989. Children dancing with scarves show how colors are combined.

McKissack, Patricia. *Mirandy and Brother Wind*. Art by Jerry Pinkney. Knopf, 1988. Mirandy wants the wind to join her in the cakewalk dance contest.

Martin, Bill, Jr., and John Archambault. *Barn Dance!* Art by Ted Rand. Holt, 1986. A rhythmic frolic as the animals hold a barn dance.

Schumaker, Ward. *Dance!* Art by the author. Harcourt, 1996. Animals cavort across the double spreads demonstrating their dancing skills.

# Animal Cracker Puppets

Easy, fast, and a treat, too. My favorite American present to bring from the United States to friends overseas is a box of animal crackers. I think of them as a truly American gift.

**YOU WILL NEED**
animal crackers

nylon fish line

cellophane, masking, or strapping tape

**PREPARATION**
All you have to do to make the animal crackers into puppets is affix a piece of nylon fish line to the back of the cracker. Use cellophane, masking, or strapping tape.

**PRESENTATION**
Dangle the animals as string marionettes to present animal poetry or introduce animal stories. The following poems work perfectly.

## Animal Crackers / People Crackers

*David McCord*

Animal crackers
Animal crackers! I ate them years
Before you did. It now appears
That indian crackers and cowboy cousins
Are eaten by millions dozens.
These new ones may look good to you,
But I am useter to the zoo.

People Crackers
People crackers! Or don't you know
They make them now for dogs, just so
That poor old Rover can enjoy
A little girl, a little boy,
While you are munching if you please
On lions, tigers, chimpanzees;
On mean hyenas full of laughs.

## Graham Cracker Animals 1-2-3

*Nancy White Carlstrom*

Graham Cracker Animals
1-2-3

Marching in a straight line
Marching to the sea.

Graham Cracker Animals
Here's one more,

Following the others
Now there are four.

Graham Cracker Animals
All climbing up,

Dancing in a circle
Around my blue cup.

Graham Cracker Animals
On a white sea,

Sailing in a silver spoon
Coming home to me.

Graham Cracker Animals
Slipping in a rush,

Tumble in the milky deep
Graham Cracker Mush.

# Fish
# Marionettes

I purchase amazing marionettes in countries around the world, but many of my experiences with them have been frustrating. Marionettes are operated with strings, which take more practice and skill than working with simpler puppets. Naturally, when I have new marionettes I want to play with them, but since I'm not a very tidy housekeeper, the strings of my puppets are often hopelessly tangled.

## Yarn Jellyfish

Here are two versions of a beginner's marionette that you can create quickly. Just one string is used. Take your pick or create your own version.

**YOU WILL NEED**
scissors
yarn (how much depends on whether you want a big or small jellyfish)
butcher paper
crayons

**PREPARATION**

Take equal lengths of yarn. (My jellyfish is made with variegated yarn and is very pretty and graceful. The jellyfish that sometimes invade the ocean in front of my home are equally pretty, but they sting.) Fold the yarn in half to make a bundle. Tie a piece of yarn around the yarn bundle at the fold to create the head. The string that ties the head also is your operating string.

*An alternative method:* Twist colored craft pipe cleaners into the shape of a jellyfish ready to attack.

### Hint

Braid the tail of your jellyfish into eight arms to form an octopus that can join the dance.

Draw an undersea scene on butcher paper as a background set for your dance.

**PRESENTATION**

Puppeteers lean over a table or bookshelf and dangle their performers over the edge, where they sway and

bump into each other to the rhythm of the poem "A Smack of Jellyfish," which your group or a single narrator recites.

---

## A Smack of Jellyfish

*A. Mifflin Lowe*

Whacking and smacking and slapping along,
it's the jellyfish singing the jellyfish song.
Saying "whoops, oops, pardon, oh please excuse me,"
they bump into each other all over the sea.
For having no feet to inhibit their motion,
they're carried about by the waves of the ocean.
And they make quite a jam when they get all that jelly
bunched up back to back and belly to belly.
So if down by the seaside you hear a loud squish,
it's surely a smack of some fat jellyfish.

## Metallic Fish

To animate the next poem, by Dahlov Ipcar, create paper fish marionettes and let them join the jellyfish in the ocean to dance.

**YOU WILL NEED**

| | |
|---|---|
| metallic paper | thread |
| glue | transparent tape |

**PREPARATION**

Design fish using metallic paper and glued-on fins. A thread attached with cellophane tape is the operating string.

**PRESENTATION**
Don't worry if the fish twists in performance. The transparent tape and string will not be seen by the audience.

## Fishes' Evening Song

*Dahlov Ipcar*

Flip flop,
Flip flap.
Slip slap,
Lip lap;
Water sounds,
Soothing sounds,
Soothing sounds.
We fan our fins
As we lie
Resting here
Eye to eye.
Water falls
Drop by drop.
Plip plop,
Drip drop.
Plink plunk,
Splash splish;
Fish fins fan,
Fish tails swish,
Swush, swash, swish.
This we wish . . .
Water cold,
Water clear,
Water smooth,
Just to soothe
Sleepy fish.

## Books to Share: Fish

Ehlert, Lois. *Fish Eyes: A Book You Can Count On.* Art by the author. Harcourt, 1990. Count fish plus a child up to ten.

McKissack, Patricia C. *A Million Fish . . . More or Less.* Art by Dena Schuster. Knopf, 1992. Hugh Thomas catches a million fish, more or less, in a spirited tall tale.

Pfister, Marcus. *The Rainbow Fish.* Art by the author. North–South, 1992. The shiny scaled fish gives his fins to other fish and makes friends.

Wilcox, Cathy. *Enzo the Wonderfish.* Art by the author. Tichnor, 1994. A young girl tries to teach her goldfish tricks.

# Pocket Puppets and the "Poor Old Lady" or "There Was an Old Man"

**A** pocket puppet will fascinate your children. Objects or pictures are placed in an opening in a puppet. Use a pocket puppet to present this traditional rhyme. In another version, Lori Vicker changed the old lady to an old man and extended the rhyme. Make a "unisex" body for your puppet and simply change hats to present the second rhyme.

**YOU WILL NEED**
poster board

scissors

acetate

transparent tape

animals to insert in the pocket behind the old
    man/old woman's tummy

**PREPARATION**
Using the pattern, reproduce the puppet on poster board. Cut out the tummy. Laminate the puppet. Attach a piece of acetate with the transparent tape to the back of the puppet, making a "tummy" bag into which the animals will fall.

Reproduce the animals on poster board and laminate them to make them stronger. (You will want children to help you tell the story.)

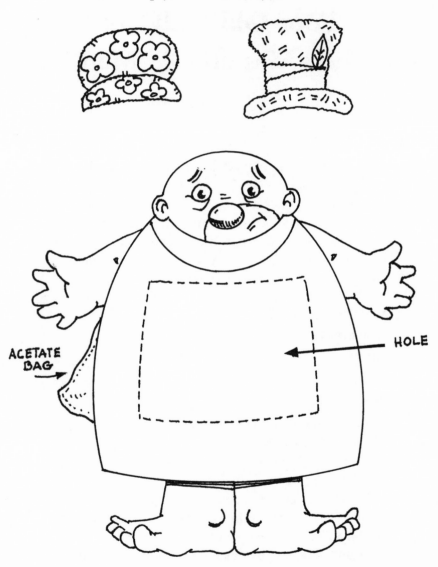

**PRESENTATION**

While you hold the puppet, children can come up one by one, each handing you one of the animals. You then drop it into the tummy. On the last line, turn your puppet sideways.

Encourage the children to chant the rhyme with you.

### Poor Old Lady

Poor old lady, she swallowed
    a fly.
I don't know why she
    swallowed a fly.
Poor old lady, I think
    she'll die.

Poor old lady, she swallowed
    a spider.
It squirmed and wriggled and
    turned inside her.
She swallowed the spider
    to catch the fly,
I don't know why she
    swallowed a fly.
Poor old lady, I think
    she'll die.

Poor old lady, she swallowed
    a bird.
How absurd! She swallowed a bird.
She swallowed the bird to catch the spider,
She swallowed the spider to catch the fly,

I don't know why she swallowed
    the fly.
Poor old lady, I think she'll die.

Poor old lady, she swallowed a cat.
Think of that! She swallowed a cat.
She swallowed the cat to catch the
    bird,
She swallowed the bird to catch
    the spider,
She swallowed the spider to catch
    the fly,
I don't know why she swallowed
    a fly.
Poor old lady, I think she'll die.

Poor old lady, she swallowed a dog.
She went the whole hog when she
    swallowed the dog.
She swallowed the dog to catch
    the cat,
She swallowed the cat to catch
    the bird,
She swallowed the bird to catch
    the spider,
She swallowed the spider to catch
    the fly,
I don't know why she swallowed
    a fly.
Poor old lady, I think she'll die.

Poor old lady, she swallowed a cow.
I don't know how she swallowed
    the cow.

She swallowed the cow to catch the dog,
She swallowed the dog to catch the cat,
She swallowed the cat to catch the bird,
She swallowed the bird to catch the spider,
She swallowed the spider to catch the fly,
I don't know why she
    swallowed a fly.
Poor old lady, I think
    she'll die.

Poor old lady, she swallowed
    a horse.
She died, of course.

## There Was an Old Man

*Lori Vicker*

There was an old man who
    swallowed a toad.
Eye-Yie-Yie!!! He may
    explode!

There was an old man who
    swallowed a bunny.
Now isn't that funny? He
    swallowed a bunny.
He swallowed the bunny to
    catch the toad.
Eye-Yie-Yie!!! He may explode!

There was an old man who swallowed a snake.
For goodness' sake! He swallowed a snake.

He swallowed the snake to catch
    the bunny.
Now isn't that funny?
    He swallowed the bunny.
He swallowed the bunny to catch
    the toad.
Eye-Yie-Yie!! He may explode!

There was an old man who
    swallowed a hawk.
It squawked and squawked as he
    swallowed the hawk!
He swallowed the hawk to catch
    the snake.
He swallowed the snake to catch
    the bunny.
Now isn't that funny?
    He swallowed the bunny.
He swallowed the bunny to catch
    the toad.
Eye-Yie-Yie!! He may explode!

There was an old man who
    swallowed a fox!
It was a great big fox wearing
    yellow socks.
He swallowed the fox to catch
    the hawk.
He swallowed the hawk to catch
    the snake.
He swallowed the snake to catch
    the bunny.
Now isn't it funny? He swallowed
    a bunny.

He swallowed the bunny to catch the toad.
Eye-Yie-Yie!! He may explode!!

There was an old man who swallowed a lion!
Without even try'in, he swallowed the lion.
He swallowed the lion
    to catch the fox.
He swallowed the fox
    to catch the hawk.
He swallowed the hawk
    to catch the snake.
He swallowed the snake
    to catch the bunny.
Now isn't it funny?
    He swallowed the bunny.
He swallowed the bunny to catch the toad.
Eye-Yie-Yie!! He may explode!!

There was an old man who swallowed a bear.
A big brown bear wearing striped underwear!!
He swallowed the bear to catch the lion.
He swallowed the lion
    to catch the fox.
He swallowed the fox
    to catch the hawk.
He swallowed the hawk
    to catch the snake.
He swallowed the snake
    to catch the bunny.
Now isn't that funny? He swallowed the bunny.
He swallowed the bunny to catch the toad.
Eye-Yie-Yie!! He may explode!!

There was an old man who swallowed a whale.
That ends this tale.

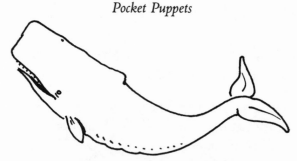

There was an old man whose name was Fred.
Guess what!!
He's . . . . . . dead!!

## Books to Share: Cumulative Food Tales

Grossman, Bill. *My Little Sister Ate One Hare*. Art by Kevin Hawkes. Crown, 1996. Bats, shrews, and ants are some of the delicacies little sister eats.

Jackson, Alison. *I Know an Old Lady Who Swallowed a Pie*. Art by Judith Byron Schachner. Dutton, 1997. Lively illustrations and funny text with a Thanksgiving theme.

Kimmel, Eric A. *The Gingerbread Man*. Art by Meagan Lloyd. Holiday, 1993. Everyone chases the gingerbread man.

Numeroff, Laura Joffe. *If You Give a Mouse a Cookie*. Art by Felicia Bond. Harper, 1985. A cumulative story relates what happens when you offer a mouse a cookie.

Polacco, Patricia. *In Enzo's Splendid Gardens*. Art by author. Philomol, 1997. A crazy old bee wreaks havoc in an outdoor restaurant.

Robard, Rose. *The Cake That Mack Ate*. Art by Maryann Kovalski. Little, 1987. A happy dog eats everything that goes into the cake and—the cake.

# Shadow
# Puppets

My mother always said, "Be friendly." Although we were warned not to speak to strangers, I do it all the time. I've met some very interesting people by being "friendly." On a plane trip to Bali, I spoke to a man from Switzerland who was on his way up to the mountains. He was searching for a site for a hiking group due the following month. By the time we landed in Bali, my husband and I had been invited to tag along on his search.

We stayed in a small mountain village. When I told the village's headman that I was curious to see a puppet show, he kindly gave me a letter to a puppeteer in a village a bike ride away.

Peter and I rode to the village and showed the letter to the first person that we found. No one in the village spoke any of the languages that we speak, but they were very hospitable. Peter and I were given a private showing of a love story with buffalo-hide shadow puppets. The puppets were given to us as a present, and they now live on my living room wall.

The memory of this extraordinary encounter has made me an enthusiastic shadow-puppet devotee.

It would be nice to take all our children on a field trip to Indonesia to observe an authentic village puppeteer, but that idea is impractical.

You can introduce your children to a less advanced, but equally interesting, form of shadow puppetry. Using materials at hand, your children can make and perform their own shadow shows.

## Making a Shadow-Puppet Stage and Screen

Shadow-puppet screens can be made from cloth, Plexiglass, or paper. The simplest shadow-puppet theater is made with the top of a cardboard carton and a sheet of translucent or tracing paper.

I timed myself making a shadow-puppet theater screen. I wanted to have a shadow-puppet dog sing "Happy Birthday" to an eighty-seven-year-old dog lover. I used the top of a box that had a lip on all four sides. I used a book as a template and traced around the book with a pencil on the inside of the box top. A paring knife from the kitchen drawer cut through the cardboard to create the opening. I taped a sheet

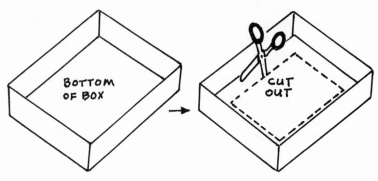

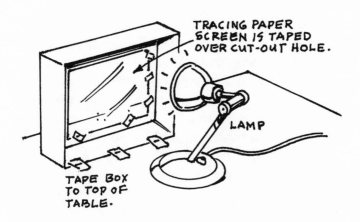

TRACING PAPER
SCREEN IS TAPED
OVER CUT-OUT HOLE.

LAMP

TAPE BOX
TO TOP OF
TABLE.

CUT OUT EYE.

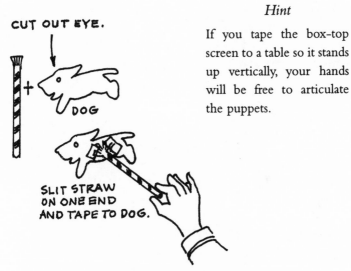

DOG

SLIT STRAW
ON ONE END
AND TAPE TO DOG.

### Hint

If you tape the box-top screen to a table so it stands up vertically, your hands will be free to articulate the puppets.

of tracing paper to the opening with masking tape. Shadow box finished. Time: eleven minutes. The dog was cut freehand from shocking-pink poster-paper—three minutes. I wanted to use a straw as the handle for my puppet, but although I searched frantically throughout the kitchen drawers (remember I was timing myself), I didn't find a straw. With a piece of discarded writing paper (from my manuscript), retrieved from the wastebasket, I made a straw by wrapping the paper around a pencil. Cutting quarter-inch vertical slits on one end of the straw, I bent the edges back so that the straw could be taped to the dog as a handle. The process took four minutes. It would have taken less time, but my first homemade straw handle was too long, and I had to cut it down.

At the party I held the screen in one hand and the dog (which looked a bit like an elderly mouse) in the other in front of a floor light (a gooseneck lamp is ideal). The dog showed pink through the tracing-paper screen.

Everyone heartily sang "Happy Birthday" as I manipulated the dog, but, of course, they were honoring the "birthday girl," not my efforts.

## Shadow-Puppet Tiger

With just one puppet, you can present these three short booktalks.

**YOU WILL NEED**

| | |
|---|---|
| tiger puppet | scissors |
| shadow screen | marker |
| paper acetate | |

**PREPARATION**

Reproduce the tiger picture. Use orange or yellow acetate (available from an art-supply shop) to cover the opening in your shadow box. Draw on the tiger's stripes with a black felt-tip marker.

**PRESENTATION**
Manipulate the tiger on the shadow screen or over-head projector as the booktalk is presented.

**Booktalk**

TIGER: Grrr! Grrr! I want Sam's new school clothes. Grrr! Grrr! I want you to read *Sam and the Tigers* by Julius Lester [Dial, 1996]. He has rewritten *Little Black Sambo*. You'll love it. Lots of action featuring me, and lively pictures by Jerry Pinkney. Grrr! Grrr!

TIGER: Have you seen Hannibal the boastful mouse? He brags that he can tickle a tiger. He did! But now my friend and I are chasing him. And when we catch him—watch out, Hannibal! Grrr! Take time out to read *Tickling Tiger* by Anna Currey, with art by the author [Barron's, 1996].

TIGER: I'm worried that the hunter will find me. I'll hide! Wait—the hunter has no gun, only a camera. This book has notes on how to save me. I'm endangered. Grrr! Grrr! The book is *Tiger* by Judy Allen, with art by Tudor Humphries [Candlewick, 1992].

# *Shadow Play*

Try creating your own outline shapes of a man, woman, and props to use with a shadow-puppet screen. This skit will also work with any puppets and stage you choose.

**CHARACTERS**
Wife
Husband

**PROPS**
pot
vegetables: carrot,
    celery, potato,
    parsley, onion,
    tomato, turnip
salt shaker
pepper shaker

## Soup, Soup, Soup

WIFE: It's Saturday, I don't have to go to work.

HUSBAND: I'm happy to stay home. Let's spend the afternoon making a vegetable soup for dinner.

WIFE: What a good idea. I love soup, and I love to cook with you.

HUSBAND: Here is a pot filled with water. I'll put it on the stove.

WIFE: I'll chop, chop, chop this carrot.

HUSBAND: I'll slice, slice, slice this celery.

WIFE: I'll dice, dice, dice this potato.

HUSBAND: I'll snip, snip, snip this parsley.

WIFE: I'll mince, mince, mince this onion.

HUSBAND: I'll mash, mash, mash this tomato.

WIFE: I'll crush, crush, crush this turnip.

HUSBAND: Preparing the soup has taken all afternoon. What fun!

WIFE: I've enjoyed it, too.

HUSBAND: While we wait for the soup to cook, I'll give you a kiss.

[Puppets *kiss*]

WIFE: And I'll give you a kiss.

[Puppets *kiss*]

HUSBAND: The soup is ready to eat.

WIFE: Let's eat.

HUSBAND: Oh no! I love to chop, slice, dice, snip, mince, mash, and crush to make the soup, but I hate vegetables. We will give the soup to our neighbors, and we'll have something our own parents would consider unhealthy. How about hot dogs and baked beans?

**Books to Share: Soup**

Brenner, Barbara. *Group Soup.* Art by Lynn Munsinger. Viking, 1992. Rhoda discovers that pitching in to help make group soup is fun.

Brown, Marcia. *Stone Soup.* Art by the author. Scribner's, 1947. Three tired soldiers teach the townspeople how to make a delicious soup with just a stone.

Desimini, Lisa. *Moon Soup.* Art by the author. Hyperion, 1993. Use a variety of unusual ingredients to make it, and realize that moon soup must be eaten while sitting on the moon.

Everitt, Betsy. *Mean Soup.* Art by the author. Harcourt, 1992. Horace is cranky until he makes mean soup with his mother.

Martin, Antoinette Truglio. *Famous Seaweed Soup.* Art by Nadine Bernard Westcott. Whitman, 1993. A little girl gathers the ingredients from the sea for her own seaweed soup.

Myers, Lynne Born, and Christopher Myers. *Turnip Soup*. Art by Katie Keller. Hyperion, 1994. There really is a dragon in the cellar where the vegetables for the soup are kept.

Orgel, Doris. *Button Soup*. Art by Paul Estrada. Bantam, 1994. RagTag Meg helps the whole neighborhood make button soup.

Rattigan, Jama Kim. *Dumpling Soup*. Art by Lillian Hsu-Flanders. Little, 1993. In Hawaii a Korean American family celebrates the new year with dumplings.

Temple, Frances. *Tiger Soup*. Art by the author. Orchard, 1994. In a story from Jamaica, Anansi tricks Tiger into leaving his soup.

# Moon Tale

When you admire the moon, do you see a face—the man in the moon—or a rabbit?

**YOU WILL NEED**
acetate

scissors

**PREPARATION**
Use the provided outline shapes to create the characters for a shadow-puppet production. Tell the following story to the group. Let the children reproduce the characters or create their own.

**PRESENTATION**
As the players manipulate the characters and props on the shadow screen or overhead projector, they can retell the story in their own words.

**CHARACTERS**

| | |
|---|---|
| Man in the Moon | Monkey |
| Fox | Rabbit |

**PROPS**

| | |
|---|---|
| fire | fruit |
| fish | moon with a rabbit silhouette |

# The Rabbit in the Moon

All night long, the Man in the Moon is busy with his work. It is his job to light the earth. He has to remember if it's an evening for a new moon or a full moon. He is in charge of moving the moon on its journey around the world.

Sometimes during the day he gets a little bored. There is not much to do on the moon except to stare down through the clouds and observe the earth creatures.

For one whole week the Man in the Moon had been watching three animals that lived together in the forest. They appeared to be happy and cooperative.

"It is odd," thought the Man in the Moon, "to see a fox, a monkey, and a rabbit living in such close harmony. I would like to meet them and see for myself which one of them is the kindest."

The very next morning, when the moon was resting from her journey around the world, the Man in the Moon dressed as a simple wood gatherer and flew down to earth.

He found the three animals chatting by a fire. All three greeted the Man in the Moon with courtesy.

"May we help you?" asked the fox.

"Yes," answered the Man in the Moon. "I am hungry. Do you have any food?"

"Of course," they answered. The fox offered to fish in the river with his tail. The monkey offered to climb a tree and gather fruit.

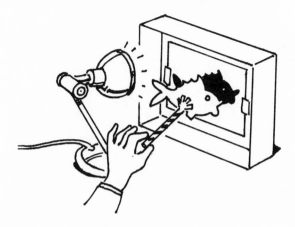

The two of them returned with fish and fruit. Now the rabbit spoke: "I would like to feed you too, sir," he said bowing. "However, my tail is too short to fish and I can't climb a tree. But you can eat *me*. I will ask my friends the fox and the monkey to build up the fire."

"No, no," said the Man in the Moon, "that will not be necessary. I have all I want to eat."

The Man in the Moon was impressed with the rabbit's generosity. He offered to take the rabbit with him back up to the moon to live. The rabbit said that he would like to visit from time to time, but would not like to live on the moon. He wanted to stay with his friends.

That is why some nights when you look at the moon, you will see a rabbit enjoying the company of the Man in the Moon.

# Puppetry Resources

## Organizations

The Puppeteers of America, Inc.
5 Cricklewood Path
Pasadena, CA 91107

Founded in 1937, the P. of A. welcomes anyone with an interest in puppetry. Member benefits include *The Puppetry Journal,* published quarterly, and *Playboard,* published bimonthly; consultant services; an audiovisual library; and the Puppetry Store. The P. of A. holds weeklong festivals biannually on college campuses across the nation and is the parent organization of a number of local puppetry guilds.

The author is grateful to Rick Morse, who compiled this list of resources. He is a puppeteer and media specialist for the Walled Lake Consolidated Schools, Walled Lake, Michigan.

UNIMA-U.S.A.
 Allelu Kurten, General Secretary
 Browning Rd.
 Hyde Park, NY 12538

 An international puppetry organization
and publisher of *Á Propos.*

# Journals

*The Puppetry Journal,* published by the Puppeteers of
America, is the major North American puppetry peri-
odical. UNIMA-U.S.A. publishes *Á Propos.* Both jour-
nals are received by members of these organizations.

# Suppliers

Maher Ventriloquial Studios
 P.O. Box 420
 Littleton, CO 80160

 Offers a variety of commercial and custom-
made puppets, as well as books, scripts, ventril-
oquistic dialogues, and construction diagrams.

The Puppetry Store
 1525 24th St. S.E.
 Auburn, WA 98002-7837
 Phone: (206) 833-8377
 Fax: (206) 939-4213

 Another service of the Puppeteers of
America, the Puppetry Store stocks more than
225 puppet-related books, pamphlets, scripts,
patterns, videos, and audiotapes.

# Videos

*Beauregard's Bottle Buddies: Plastic Bottle Puppets Made Simple.* Hands On Productions, P.O. Box 25268, Arlington, VA 22202. 1992, 30 min. Clear instructions for making clever puppets from common household items.

*Leading Kids to Books with Caroline Feller Bauer.* Library Video Network, 320 York Rd., Towson, MD 21204-5179. 1977, 30 min. Puppetry techniques and more.

# Internet

The Puppetry Home Page delivers a smorgasbord of articles, history, classified ads, and related information:

http://www-leland1.stanford.edu/~rosesage/puppetry.html

Tim Nielsen maintains a list of puppeteers' e-mail addresses. To receive a directory electronically, contact Tim at tnielsen@scf.usc.edu.

# Books for Children

Duch, Mabel. *Easy-to-Make Puppets: Step-by-Step Instructions.* Boston: Plays, 1993. Simple, quickly made puppets.

Henson, Cheryl. *The Muppets Make Puppets!* New York: Workman, 1994. Clever puppets made from scrap materials.

Mahlmann, Lewis, and David Cadwalader Jones. *Folk Tale Plays for Puppets: 13 Royalty-free Plays for Hand Puppets, Rod Puppets or Marionettes.* Boston: Plays, 1980. Suitable for production by children or adults, titles include *The Gingerbread Boy, Anansi and the Box of Stories,* and *The Little Indian Brave.*

——. *Puppet Plays for Young Players: 12 Royalty-free Plays for Hand Puppets, Rod Puppets or Marionettes.* Boston: Plays, 1974. More short adaptations of such titles as *Jack and the Beanstalk, The Frog Prince,* and *The Wizard of Oz.*

——. *Puppet Plays from Favorite Stories: Eighteen Royalty-free Plays for Hand Puppets, Rod Puppets or Marionettes.* Boston: Plays, 1977. This volume includes *Cinderella, The Three Little Pigs,* and *Beauty and the Beast.*

Renfro, Nancy. *Puppet Shows Made Easy!* Austin, Tex.: Nancy Renfro Studios, 1984. From writing the play, to building the puppets and stage, to giving the performance, older children (and adults) will find this a valuable resource.

## Books for Adults

Abbe, Dorothy. *The Dwiggins Marionettes: A Complete Experimental Theatre in Miniature.* Boston: Plays, 1970. One man's experiments with puppetry for adult audiences.

Anderson, Dee. *Amazingly Easy Puppet Plays.* Chicago: ALA, 1997. Ready-to-use scripts for preschool through third-grade audiences.

Baird, Bil. *The Art of the Puppet.* New York: Macmillan, 1965. Lavishly illustrated history of world puppetry.

Bauer, Caroline Feller. *Caroline Feller Bauer's New Handbook for Storytellers.* Chicago: ALA, 1993. "A gold mine of ideas for thematic programs, creative dramatics, booktalks, puppetry, magic."— *NJEA Review.*

Beaton, Mabel, and Les Beaton. *Marionettes: A Hobby for Everyone.* New York: Crowell, 1948. Dallas: Dallas Puppet Theater Pr., 1989. Comprehensive discussion of marionette making and play production.

Champlin, Connie. *Storytelling with Puppets.* Rev. ed. Chicago: ALA, 1997. Updating the Nancy Renfro–Connie Champlin classic, a complete repertory for storytellers, whether new or experienced puppeteers.

Chesse, Bruce, and Beverly Armstrong. *Puppets from Polyfoam: Spongees.* Portland, Oreg.: Puppet Concepts, 1990. Step-by-step instructions for making expressive mouth (Muppet-type) puppets.

Currell, David. *The Complete Book of Puppet Theatre.* London: A & C Black, 1985. Construction of all types of puppets and stages, plus chapters on production. Beautifully illustrated.

Fling, Helen. *Marionettes: How to Make and Work Them.* New York: Dover, 1973. Good guide for older children and adults.

Hunt, Tamara, and Nancy Renfro. *Puppetry in Early Childhood Education.* Austin, Tex.: Nancy Renfro Studios, 1982. Exhaustive guide to puppetry as an educational resource.

Renfro, Nancy. *A Puppet Corner in Every Library.* Austin, Tex.: Nancy Renfro Studios, 1978. Puppet corners, library instruction, storytelling, and more.

Sims, Judy. *Puppets for Dreaming and Scheming: A Puppet Source Book.* Santa Barbara, Calif.: Learning Works, 1988. One of the very best titles dealing with puppetry in schools and libraries.

Sinclair, Anita. *The Puppetry Handbook.* Castlemaine, Vic. Austral.: Richard Lee, 1995. Packed with creative ideas for making and using all types of puppets.

VanSchuyver, Jan. *Storytelling Made Easy with Puppets.* Phoenix: Oryx, 1993. Using puppets to introduce books, lead songs, and tell stories. The section "Puppetry Hints and Resources" alone is worth the price of the book.

**C**aroline **Feller Bauer** has traveled in more than one hundred countries, lecturing in over sixty of them. She is well known around the world for her lively show-and-tell lectures to children, parents, and professionals in which she features creative ideas for bringing children and books together.

A member of the Puppeteers of America and the Miami Puppet Guild, she is the recipient of many awards. She is the author of the classic *Caroline Feller Bauer's New Handbook for Storytellers* (ALA, 1993), *Leading Kids to Books through Magic* (ALA, 1996), and seventeen other books for children and adults.